COMBAT LEGEND
AVRO LANCASTER

Harry Holmes

Airlife

Copyright © 2002 Airlife Publishing Ltd

Text written by Harry Holmes
Profile illustrations drawn by Dave Windle
Cover painting by Jim Brown – The Art of Aviation Co. Ltd
First published in the UK in 2002
by Airlife Publishing Ltd

British Library Cataloguing-in-Publication Data
A catalogue record for this book
is available from the British Library

ISBN 1 84037 376 8

Printed in Hong Kong

Contact us for a free catalogue that describes the complete range of Airlife
books for aviation enthusiarts.

Airlife Publishing Ltd
101 Longden Road, Shrewsbury, SY3 9EB, England
E-mail: sales@airlifebooks.com
Website: www.airlifebooks.com

Contents

An AEC Matador bowser stands ready to fuel a Lancaster of No. 50 Squadron at Skellingthorpe. The crews could usually guess the target by the amount of fuel being delivered. The aircraft's maximum fuel capacity of 2,154 Imp gal usually meant a trip to 'The Big City', Berlin, or other long-range targets.

Lancaster Timeline

20 February 1940
Avro discusses Manchester aircraft powered by four Rolls-Royce Merlin engines with Air Ministry

9 January 1941
Maiden flight of BT308, now named Lancaster

26 November 1941
First Flight of DT810, the Prototype Lancaster Mk II, powered by Bristol Hercules radial engines

24 December 1941
No. 44 Squadron RAF receives first Lancasters

3/4 March 1942
First operation, to lay mines

10/11 March 1942
First bombing operation in raid on Essen

17 April 1942
Daylight raid on Augsburg

16/17 May 1943
Operation *Chastise*. The attack on the Rhur Dams

15/16 September 1943
First use of the 12,000lb HC (High Capacity) bomb in an attack on the Dortmund-Ems Canal at Ladbergen

7/8 October 1943
No. 101 Squadron Lancasters used the 'Airborne Cigar' communications jamming system operationally for the first time

22/23 October 1943
'Corona', German-speaking British radio operators used to confuse enemy controllers, used for the first time

3/4 November 1943
First full-scale test of G-H blind-bombing radar equipment in attack on Düsseldorf

10 November 1943
H_2S Mk III aircraft delivered to Nos 83 and 97 (PFF) Squadrons

18/19 November 1943
The Battle of Berlin opens with an attack by 440 Lancasters

8/9 June 1944
The first attack using the 12,000lb 'Tallboy' bomb was made against the Saumur railway tunnel with great success

17/18 September 1944
Lancasters flew diversionary operations in support of Operation *Market Garden*, the airborne assault to capture the bridges at Arnhem and Nijmegen in Holland

12 November 1944
Flying from Lossiemouth, Scotland, Lancasters sank the battleship *Tirpitz* which was anchored near Tromsø, Norway

12 March 1945
Bomber Command launched its largest raid on a single target during the whole of the World War Two when 1,108 aircraft, including 748 Lancasters, attacked Dortmund

14 March 1945
First operational use of the 22,000lb 'Grand Slam' bomb in an attack against the railway viaduct at Bielefeld

25 April 1945
Hitler's 'Eagle's Nest' lodge at Berchtesgaden and the nearby SS barracks were bombed by a force of 359 Lancasters and 16 Mosquitos

25/26 April 1945
The last heavy bomber raid of the war saw 107 Lancasters of No. 5 Group (the first operator of the Lancaster) attack the large oil refinery at Tønsberg in southern Norway

29 April 1945
Lancasters joined USAAF Boeing B-17 Flying Fortresses in Operation *Manna*, the air dropping of food to the starving inhabitants of western Holland

2 February 1946
Lancaster Mk I (FE) TW910 built by Armstrong Whitworth, was the last Lancaster to be delivered to the RAF

20 February 1954
The last overseas-based Lancaster, RF273 of No. 38 Squadron, returned to UK from Malta

15 October 1956
The Avro Lancaster was officially withdrawn from RAF service in a ceremony held at St Mawgan, Cornwall. Lancasters continued to serve for some time longer in Canada, France and Argentina

1. Prototypes and Development

The origin of the Avro Lancaster can be traced back to September 1936 when the Air Ministry issued Specification P.13/36 which called for a large twin-engined monoplane bomber which would be capable of alternative bomb load and range performance combinations, without modifications to the bomb bay or fuel capacity. Other requirements were the capability of dive bombing, a high cruising speed, minimal internal changes for troop carrier operations and, in its primary role, a maximum bomb load of 8,000 lb and provision for two torpedoes for anti-shipping attacks. A strengthened fuselage was to be investigated as the Royal Aircraft Establishment (RAE) at Farnborough was examining the possibility of a catapult system for launching aircraft from airfields which had been disabled by bombing. The powerplant for this new aircraft was to be the new Rolls-Royce Vulture, a 24-cylinder X-type engine which was under development.

Besides Avro, five other aircraft companies tendered their designs for the P.13/36 specification, but it was A.V. Roe & Company Limited with the Type 679 and Handley Page Limited with the H.P.56, which were the two successful companies receiving orders for prototype aircraft. The radical new engine was beset by numerous problems causing Handley Page to change its design to take four Merlin engines with the new aircraft being designated H.P.57, later to be known as the Halifax. The Avro 679 was given the name Manchester.

Despite the Vulture's reported development problems, Avro's chief designer, Roy Chadwick, decided to continue with the original design plans. Although the news from Rolls-Royce at Derby on bench running and early flight trials was not good he received assurances that things would improve. However, continuing difficulties and delays with the engine threw his plans into confusion. The Manchester's maiden flight was eventually completed at Ringway on 25 July

The prototype Avro Type 679 Manchester awaits its first flight in the Ringway sunshine on 25 July 1939.

Above: This Manchester Mk I, now with a central fin to improve directional stability, flew operationally before going to a conversion unit. R5771 survived to become the instructional airframe 3746M.

Below: In a similar view to that above, the prototype Lancaster, BT308, shows its large central fin. The Boscombe Down trials showed the need for yet more directional improvement.

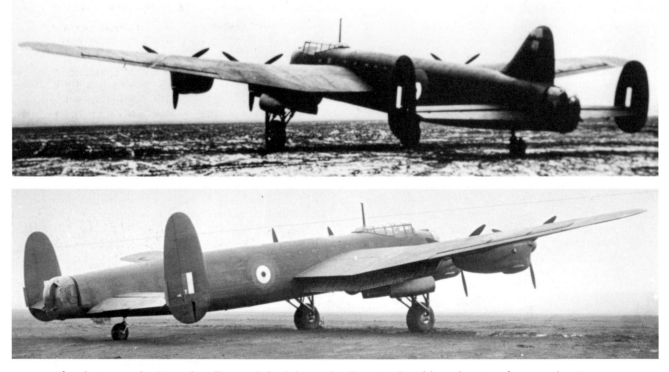

After the Boscombe Down handling trials had shown the directional problem, the aircraft returned to Avro at Ringway to have its tailplane extended and larger fins and rudders fitted. The central fin was also deleted at this time. Just six weeks later, BT308 was back at Boscombe with the now familiar twin-finned arrangement. The improvement was so significant that it was retrofitted to its predecessor, with that type becoming known as the Manchester Mk IA. A Manchester undercarriage was used on BT308, but larger wheels were soon adopted.

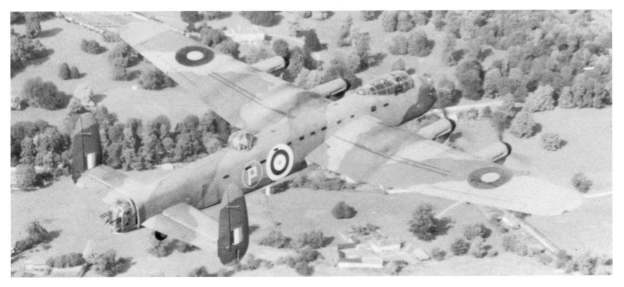

The second prototype Lancaster, DG595, was fully productionised by the time of its maiden flight on 13 May 1941. A delay in the A&AEE's testing programme at Boscombe proved a bonus for Roy Chadwick as he used the time to improve the Lancaster's systems for ease of maintenance. The aircraft is shown here during a flight in June 1941.

1939 with chief test pilot H.A. 'Sam' Brown at the aircraft's controls.

Despite Chadwick's faith in the Vulture, he nevertheless had his design team investigate the possibility of a four-engined replacement for the Avro 679 Manchester under the Type Numbers 680, 681 and 682, all of which were serious studies. The engines under consideration were all of Bristol manufacture with the Hercules, Taurus and Pegasus being included in the design

studies. Alternatives for a twin-engined Manchester Mk II were the Bristol Centaurus and the Napier Sabre.

By the end of January 1940 1,200 Manchesters had been ordered from Avro by the Air Ministry, but only 158 of these were ever delivered as the troubled Vulture, one of Rolls-Royce's few failures, was to be cancelled. It was considered that the effort in time and manpower to continue developing and improving the Vulture would be

The first production Lancaster Mk I, L7527, seen here ready for its maiden flight at Woodford on 31 October 1941, made extensive use of Manchester components. After Boscombe trials and service with a conversion unit, the aircraft joined No. 15 Squadron and was lost on the night of 26/27 March 1944 in a raid on Essen.

Powered by Bristol Hercules VI radials, the Lancaster Mk II prototype flew for the first time on 26 November 1941. The A&AEE's evaluation of DT810 was so successful that a second prototype Mk II, which was already on order, was not required.

wasted, especially as the Merlin was proving to be excellent, and more powerful versions were already in the pipeline. The decision to cancel the Vulture left Avro with a fine airframe and also a pressing need to find an alternative engine to power it.

The proposed performance of a four-Merlin Manchester Mk III had already been discussed with the Air Ministry on 20 February 1940. Polite interest had been shown, but Merlin engines were urgently needed to power Spitfire and Hurricane fighters for defence and it was these aircraft which had to have priority.

Roy (later Sir Roy) Dobson, the Avro managing director, was already one step ahead as, on 1 April 1940, he had appointed Stuart Davies to take charge of the Experimental Department to supervise the introduction of a new bomber. The new type, the Avro 683, was to have the minimum of change from the production Manchester which, by that time, had already received approval for a proposed wing span increase from 80 ft to 90 ft. It was also planned to increase the tailplane span. Rolls-Royce was already keeping Chadwick informed on the progress being made on the installation of the Merlin into a Bristol Beaufighter and, without modification, these Beaufighter power units

could be fitted into the outer mainplanes of the new bomber, which had a proposed wing span of 100 ft. The centre section of the Avro 679 would remain unchanged, but with modifications to the engine mountings and nacelle panels to house the Merlin. Stuart Davies was convinced that the retention of the Type 679's centre section was crucial in meeting the tight schedule when the production lines were later changed over from the Manchester to the new bomber.

Political manoeuvring

However, that change was still in the future as Roy Dobson met William (later Sir William) Farren at the Ministry of Aircraft Production. Farren was enthusiastic about the project, advising Dobson that great efforts should be made to convince the Air Ministry that the production of the Merlin-powered aircraft would pose no significant problems. On 28 June 1940, Air Chief Marshal Sir Wilfrid Freeman, Air Member for Production, visited Avro's huge new factory at Chadderton to view production of the Manchester. As Chadwick already knew that the Vulture was to be cancelled it was important to present the new bomber's potential to Freeman. After this visit Farren wrote to Dobson stressing that the use of Manchester components was the only way to receive approval for the Type 683 and to get the new bomber into service as early as possible. Of course, Dobson and Chadwick were working on that very thing.

On 29 July 1940, Dobson received a shock when a letter from Sir Wilfrid Freeman stated that plans for the Manchester Mk III should be dropped immediately as Avro was to build the Handley Page Halifax instead! After numerous telephone calls, the still shaken Dobson was on his way to London and fewer than twenty-four hours after receiving the letter he, together with Chadwick, was in the office of Patrick Henessy at the Ministry of Aircraft Production. After a presentation on the great potential of the Manchester Mk III, Henessy, with Dobson and Chadwick in tow, went to see Captain R.N. Liptrott who was adviser to the Ministry. Liptrott, an ex-naval aviator, was extremely taken with the duo's case for the aircraft and in a memo to all concerned endorsed the Avro 683, 'There is no reason that this aircraft with four Merlins should not have the same performance as the twin-engined Manchester.' As is now known, that was a masterly understatement, but it did serve to get the go-ahead for Avro to complete two prototypes by July 1941.

Because of the Dobson and Chadwick approach and the subsequent approval for the prototypes, moves were afoot to frustrate Avro at every turn. One ploy was to find any number of reasons to delay the provision of the four Merlins, but never one to be denied, Dobson contacted his friend Mr E.W. Hives (later Lord Hives) at Rolls-Royce and it was through his

good offices and a little of the 'old pals act' that the four Merlins were forthcoming. It was a bonus that the engines were complete Beaufighter units, which made the fitment ideal for Chadwick's design.

Dobson informed Davies that the two prototypes had to be flying by 31 May 1941, but of course, Davies was not to know that that date was two months ahead of the actual date given to Dobson! Davies prepared a plan which would see the first prototype flying by 31 December 1940, to the delight of the two Roys.

Lancaster first flight

The construction of the prototype went as planned. So well in fact, that Davies was able to tell Dobson that the aircraft should be cleared to fly by Christmas Eve 1940. A timetable was set and it was planned that on 5 and 6 December the completed aircraft would be dismantled at Chadderton ready for transportation to the Avro experimental flight hangar at Ringway Airport. The aircraft was dismantled on time, but during a German air raid bombs were dropped on the

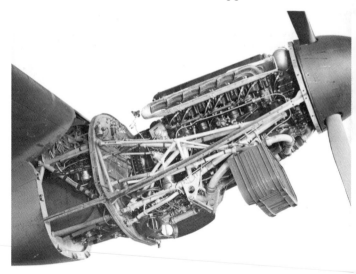

Right: The Packard Merlin engine as fitted to the port inner (No. 2) position on W4114. The Rolls-Royce Merlin was fitted with SU carburettors while the American Packard Merlin had the Bendix Stromberg pressure-injected type.

Below: A Lancaster makes a low pass over Woodford during a test flight early in 1942. Another awaits its crew on the ramp, while in the background are two Manchesters at Woodford for their conversions from Mk I to IA standard.

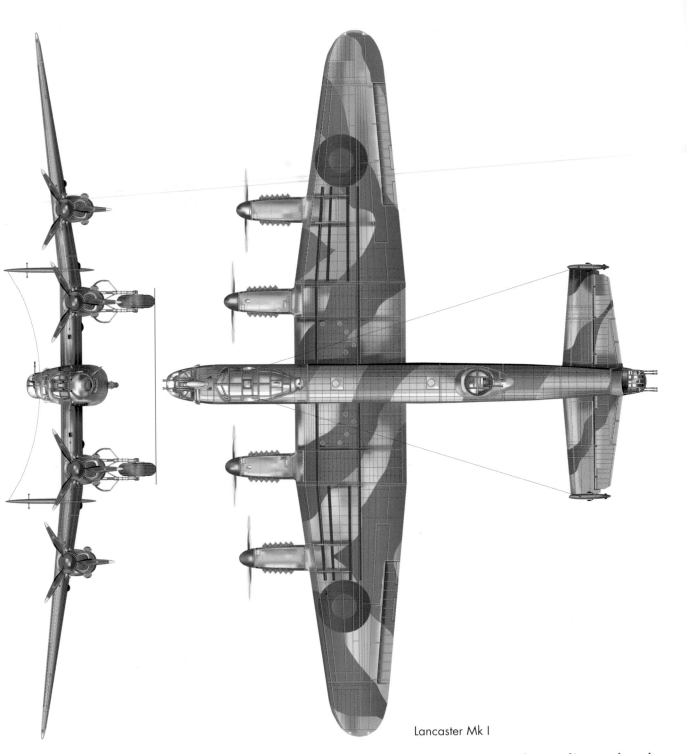

Lancaster Mk I

airport resulting in a precautionary delay. The schedule was on course again by 16 December, but reports of substantial problems with the hydraulic system of the in-service Manchesters forced Chadwick to seek a complete change in the type of pipes and couplings already equipping the prototype. Dobson immediately ordered that this work be carried out and consoled Davies with the fact that his original date of New Year's Eve could still be met.

One of the most dramatic changes to the basic Lancaster airframe came in the early months of 1943, with the requirement for the aircraft to be modified to carry and deliver 'Upkeep', Dr Barnes Wallis's mine. This 'bouncing bomb', used to attack the great dams of the German Ruhr in Operation *Chastise*, was delivered by Lancasters of the newly-formed No. 617 Squadron on the night of 16/17 May 1943. The aircraft pictured, ED817, took part in the early test drops of the weapon at Reculver, Kent, but did not take part in the attack, possibly due to damage received in the trials when heavy spray and metal splinters hit the aircraft.

The prototype, serial number BT308, was rolled out for engine runs on 28 December 1940, but after a more than normal number of adjustments it was not until 4 January 1941 that the final engine runs were completed and the aircraft was cleared to fly. However, the January weather then turned against Avro with low cloud, drizzle and the occasional fog hanging over Ringway.

On 9 January 1941 the skies cleared sufficiently for Avro chief test pilot Sam Brown, assisted by his deputy Bill Thorn, to carry out the first flight. Still known to all at that time as the Avro 683 Manchester Mk III, the Clearance to Fly Design Certificate clearly states that the aircraft is a LANCASTER! The name was selected by Chadwick as a tribute to the capital town of Lancashire and was wholeheartedly approved by Roy Dobson, a Yorkshireman! The 40-minute flight was described as 'marvellous' by the pilots, although statements like this are always to be expected after the first flight of any prototype. The new machine's reliability was really tested by nine rigorous flights which took place over the following 12 days. Before the aircraft departed for service trials at the Aircraft & Armament Experimental Establishment (A&AEE) at Boscombe Down, Wiltshire, on 27 January 1941, Roy Dobson received word that the name Lancaster had been officially approved.

The prototype had twin fins and rudders supplemented by a large central fin and although early handling trials were successful it was recommended that larger twin fins were fitted, while the centre fin was deleted. Despite this requirement, early flight tests at Boscombe had convinced the Air Ministry of the aircraft's great potential and the original contracts with Avro and Metropolitan-Vickers (Metro-Vick) for the Manchester were soon amended to be for the Lancaster. It had already been decided that No. 5 Group of Bomber Command would be the first to operate the new bomber and, as early as 1 February 1941, Air Vice Marshal N.H. Bottomley, AOC, No. 5 Group flew the prototype at Boscombe Down.

Airframe changes

The change of tail configuration required the aircraft to return to Ringway, and the first flight after this modification took place on 21 February 1941. On the following morning, Sam Brown flew BT308 with the two port engines stopped, demonstrating that the larger rudders could keep the aircraft flying perfectly straight.

The second prototype, DG595, was completed at Chadderton on 23 April 1941 and this aircraft was fully productionised. Just three weeks later, on 13 May 1941, the test pilots Brown and Thorn made its first flight. Sam Brown reported to

In wartime Woodford's ramp at the Flight Sheds was always full of Lancasters awaiting test flights or delivery and this scene in August 1944 was no exception. Both Lancasters on the left of the photograph had short lives after being cleared by test pilot Ken Cook on the 4th of that month (PD261, nearest) and on the 11th (PD269) respectively. The former was shot down on the night of 29/30 August with the loss of its crew while attacking Stettin with No. 166 Squadron as AS-S, having flown just 47 hours. The latter, as WP-Q of No. 90 Squadron, had completed 135 hours when it too was lost, this time on 31 October 1944 during a daylight raid on Bottrop. Again the entire crew was lost.

Chadwick that, 'it was an absolute delight to fly' and the aircraft was soon cleared to join A&AEE for service trials. After the elation, it came as a blow to Avro to hear that the Boscombe Down team already had a number of new aircraft desiring their expert attention and the second Lancaster could not be accepted, at least for the time being. The delay, although troublesome, proved to be a bonus for Chadwick as he had already identified a number of areas which could be improved. After discussions with Roy Dobson, Chadwick arranged for DG595 to be flown to Woodford where the aircraft was positioned in the 'Finals' area, and after detailing sixty of his top draughtsmen to make the journey from Chadderton, he stationed them around the aircraft. He wanted a complete review of the Lancaster and its systems and a number of changes were made, including

significant ones for ease of maintenance. All of the changes were approved by the Ministry, but it was 16 August 1941 before the aircraft could be flown to Boscombe Down.

Manchester discontinued

The two prototypes were already flying by the time Avro received the contract for them on 15 July 1941. A further two prototypes were also included in this contract with the two extra aircraft, DT810 and DT812, being fitted with Bristol Hercules radial engines in place of the Merlins as a safeguard against a shortage of the Rolls-Royce engine. The first prototype of the radial-engined version, to be known as the Lancaster Mk II, took to the air for its maiden flight on 26 November 1941. It proved to be good enough to complete the Mk II trials and the second prototype was not required.

An annular cowling was used for the Merlin 85s which powered the Lancaster Mk VI, as this engine was the Type 65 fitted with an auxiliary gearbox drive. This aircraft, JB675, saw service with a number of squadrons although no operational flying was carried out. Eventually it returned to Rolls-Royce before being scrapped in July 1948.

As the serious troubles with the Manchester continued, production ended with the balance of the order for that type being requested as Lancasters, with 43 from the parent company and 57 from Metropolitan-Vickers making the changeover. The first production aircraft, L7527, first flew from Woodford on 31 October 1941.

The continuing trials at the A&AEE showed some weakness in the Lancaster wing tips and this was confirmed later in early squadron service. The aircraft's wing span was increased to 102 ft with aircraft in build modified during manufacture, while the few which were ready for service were retrofitted at Waddington.

The Lancaster Production Group, thrown into disarray over the cancellation of the Manchester, had to gear up to build Lancasters. The Metropolitan-Vickers contract had already received approval for the changeover and now, following the great potential of the Lancaster, new orders were placed with Armstrong Whitworth Aircraft, Vickers-Armstrong and Austin Motors (later known as Austin Aero). Short Brothers of Belfast was also scheduled to build 200 Lancasters at a later date, but as the war began to progress favourably these aircraft were not required. Avro at Chadderton was at full stretch, while Woodford was learning to cope with the assembly of bombers on two production lines using Chadderton-manufactured sections, and a third line was established for similar sections arriving from Metro-Vick at Trafford Park, Manchester. On 6 June 1941 the parent company received a contract for 454 Lancasters with the promise of further substantial orders. This seemed a little strange as it was not until five weeks later that the contract for the first two prototypes arrived on Roy Dobson's desk! Production would have to increase rapidly and the Avro shadow factory at Yeadon (now Leeds-Bradford Airport) was mobilised to build the Lancaster.

Alternative engines

With Yeadon being the third factory to produce Lancasters and with other plants gearing up to commence production, Rolls-Royce was becoming concerned that the Merlin engines could not be turned out at a rate to satisfy the ever-increasing demand for its excellent powerplant. The first solution to the problem was the use of alternative engines and the fitting of the Bristol Hercules into the Lancaster Mk II was already in the pipeline. The second solution was for the production of the Merlin in North America and this was undertaken by the Packard Motor Corporation. The original US-built engine was designated Merlin 28. It was based on the British Merlin 22, but had a number of slight differences including carburation. The Merlin itself underwent various improvements and power increases, with the Merlin 22 rated at 1,280 hp, the Merlin 24 giving 1,620 hp and the Packard-built Merlin 28 with Bendix carburettors rated at 1,300 hp. The 1,390-hp US version of the Merlin 22 was known as the Merlin 38, while the Merlin 224 was the Packard-built Merlin 24.

The first development trials of the Packard

The first Canadian-built Lancaster, Mk X KB700, arrived in England in September 1943. After examination by the A&AEE and Avro, with the aircraft seen here at Woodford, the machine was delivered to No. 405 (RCAF) Squadron on 5 October 1943 and was given the name *Ruhr Express*. It was later transferred to No. 419 (RCAF) Squadron, but was destroyed when it overshot on landing at Middleton St George on 2 January 1945.

Merlin 28-powered Lancaster began in August 1942 using two Mk I aircraft, R5849 and W4114, with the latter being designated as the prototype Lancaster Mk III. The Mk III had an almost identical performance to the Mk I, but was given the new designation because of its different servicing requirements, although both types came off the same production line without any problems and were built to their particular Mark by the arrival of the new engine batches at the manufacturers. In squadron service it was found that the Mk IIIs were more economical on fuel.

The Packard Motor Corporation also shipped its Merlins over the border into Canada where Victory Aircraft of Malton, Toronto, had been established by the National Steel Corporation of Canada to build Lancasters under the designation Mk X. The first Canadian-built aircraft, KB700, made its first flight on 6 August 1943 and was ferried to England for development work on 17 September 1943. This aircraft was later supplied to No. 405 Squadron

on 5 October for operational assessment, but the first unit to become fully operational with the Mk X was No. 419 (Moose) Squadron, at Middleton St George in April 1944.

Lancaster Mk II in production

Production of the radial-engined Mk II with the 1,650-hp Bristol Hercules VI had been set up at the Armstrong Whitworth plants in the Coventry area with final assembly at Baginton. The Lancaster Mk II featured a bomb bay extension which had been evaluated on the second prototype Mk I. A ventral FN 64 gun turret was fitted behind the bomb bay and although it was only aft facing, the turret could be turned through an arc of 100° on either side of the centreline. The Mk II was later given more power with the fitting of the Bristol Hercules XVI which increased its speed to that of the Merlin Lancasters, but the radial-engined machine was generally restricted to a service ceiling of just over 15,000 ft at maximum weight. The Mk II also had a higher fuel consumption than the Merlin-powered aircraft. The first unit

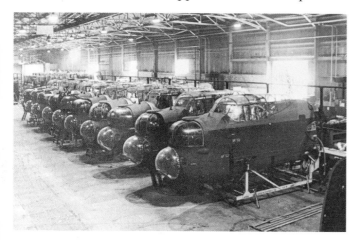

Left: Armstrong Whitworth Aircraft of Coventry produced over 1,300 Lancasters, including 300 radial-engined Mk IIs. This image shows the nose section production line at the Baginton plant in June 1944. The nearest aircraft, NF921, was allocated to No. 50 Squadron on 13 August 1944. Sadly, just over two weeks later, on 28/29 August 1944, it was lost without trace following an attack on Königsberg.

Below: Back at Ringway in October 1943 is the transport conversion CF-CMS, which was later used on the Dorval to Prestwick transatlantic route. The aircraft is a far cry from its time as R5727 which went to Canada as pattern for the Victory built Lancasters.

to operate the Mk II was No. 61 Squadron, which had just one flight equipped with this variant from October 1942 until the following March. The first fully operational unit was No. 115 Squadron which flew the Mk II from March 1943 to April 1944.

The establishment of the Pathfinder Force (PFF) on 15 August 1942 saw the build-up of squadrons joining this elite unit in No. 8 Group. The Lancaster Mk Is, and later the Mk IIIs, used on pathfinder duties required no changes in the bomb bay in order to carry the special bombs which were used as Target Indicators (TI), but were constantly updated with the latest in navigation and bombing aids.

The development of the Lancaster continued with the introduction of the Mk VI in a programme to improve the aircraft's performance by fitting the 1,750-hp Merlin 85, an engine that was developed for use on the proposed Lancaster Mk IV and Mk V which later

The requirement for long-range operations against the Japanese saw the introduction of the rather ugly 'Saddle Tank' installation. Two aircraft, HK541 and SW244, were allocated for the modification with a proposed all-up weight of 72,000 lb, but the war ended as exhaustive trials were under way. The first aircraft had served with No. 115 Squadron as KO-P, but SW244, pictured here, was a new aircraft which had made its first flight from Woodford as a standard Mk I on 5 December 1944 in the hands of on-loan RAF test pilot Squadron Leader Viatkin.

Above: The Avro (Yeadon) built SW368 was converted to a lifeboat-equipped ASR.Mk III and served with a number of squadrons. It was found that the standard H$_2$S radar was not suitable for sea-search duties and a maritime version was developed. With the maritime recce role taking priority SW368 was modified to GR.Mk III configuration, while retaining the capability of carrying the airborne lifeboat. After storage the aircraft was sold to the scrapman in July 1956.

Right: Armstrong Whitworth's last batch of Lancasters was completed as Mk I (FE)s including TW872 TL-D of No. 35 Squadron. The unit made an excellent impression during Operation *Lancaster*, a goodwill tour of the United States in August 1946.

The Avro Lancaster was officially retired from RAF service at St Mawgan on 15 October 1956 and here RF325, from the School of Maritime Reconnaissance, stands awaiting the hundreds of guests who marked the occasion. Despite the proud day with tributes coming from all quarters, the aircraft was then unceremoniously flown away to Wroughton and the scrapyard. The historic flight was made by the School's Wing Commander Brooks.

became known as the Lincoln Mk I and Mk II. Two Lancaster Mk IIIs were allocated to Rolls-Royce in June 1943 to serve as test-beds for the new engine with five others being subsequently converted. Four of these aircraft saw action with PFF squadrons, but as the engine had not yet been fully developed this type of aircraft was withdrawn from operations in November 1944.

In July 1943 plans were made to operate the Lancaster against the Japanese in the Far East and from October of that year two aircraft were deployed in Mauripur, India, to assess operations in tropical climates which included long-range flights, performance trials and even glider towing. It appeared that the aircraft's operational range could be a problem and Avro designed a 1,200 Imp gal fuel tank for the top decking of the fuselage from the cockpit to where the mid-upper gun turret would have been. Two aircraft were converted to the 'Saddle Tank' configuration with weights up to 72,000 lb. The first arrived in Mauripur on 8 May 1945 as news of the German surrender reached India, while the second followed on 11 August 1945 for extensive trials in India, Burma, Ceylon and Australia. Much data was obtained from these trials, but by that time a tropicalisation modification had already been devised for the standard Lancaster. Aircraft could be converted or changed during manufacture with the

designation Lancaster Mk I (FE) or Mk VII (FE) on the Austin-built machine, for the forthcoming Tiger Force. Range could be extended by means of inflight refuelling which was at that time being investigated by Flight Refuelling Limited (FRL) after many years of research. Eventually, neither the Lancaster nor the Lincoln was required to operate against Japan as the war ended before any scheme was initiated.

Post-war development continued for the Lancaster which, during wartime, was little used for anything other than bombing, at which it was supreme. However, hostilities ended, and it was decided to adopt the Lancaster for the air-sea rescue (ASR) role, with an airborne lifeboat attached to a special mounting under the bomb bay. Others were converted to General Reconnaissance (GR) aircraft with a search radar in place of the H_2S bombing aid. One interesting post-war variant was the Photographic Reconnaissance Lancaster PR.Mk I which had the front and rear turrets faired over and a variety of cameras fitted into the bomb bay for aerial survey work.

However, it is as a bomber that the Avro Lancaster will always be remembered as, with little modification to its original airframe, this great aircraft completed every task to the highest standard and is a lasting tribute to those who designed, built, maintained and flew it.

2. Operational History

As No. 5 Group of RAF Bomber Command had been given the distinction of introducing the Lancaster into service, it was No. 44 (Rhodesia) Squadron stationed at Waddington which received a much awaited Christmas present when three of the new bombers were flown in on 24 December 1941. A number of pilots from other squadrons within No. 5 Group had already flown the Lancaster at Boscombe Down and Woodford, but it was No. 44 Squadron under the impressive leadership of Wing Commander Roderick Learoyd, VC which had been selected as the first recipient. This unit had operated the Handley

A formation of Lancasters from No. 44 Squadron in September 1942. This unit introduced the type to operations and had the honour of winning the first Lancaster Victoria Cross, which was awarded to Squadron Leader J.D. Nettleton for leading the daring daylight raid on Augsburg on 17 April 1942.

One of the early Lancasters which started life as a Manchester was L7540 OL-U of No. 83 Squadron. It is seen here at Scampton in June 1942 surrounded by 'Cookies'. Interestingly, the mid-upper turret has not yet received its fairing and the aircraft shows evidence of its short stay with No. 44 Squadron as the code-letters KM-J show clearly under its new identity.

Page Hampden with success, but that type was already obsolete in the bombing role and the crews were anxious to convert to their new charge. The second unit to put the Lancaster into service was No. 97 (Straits Settlements) Squadron commanded by Wing Commander John Kynoch at Coningsby. This unit received its new aircraft on 12 January 1942 replacing the dreaded Avro Manchester. The squadron's ground crews were familiar with many of the systems of the Lancaster as they were identical to the older machine making the changeover go relatively smoothly. On 8 March 1942, No. 207 Squadron at Bottesford was the third unit to be equipped with the Lancaster.

The first operation carried out by Lancasters was on 3 March 1942 when four aircraft from No. 44 Squadron were detailed to lay mines in Heligoland Bight. The Lancasters took off from Waddington at 18.15 hours and all returned safely just five hours later.

Seven days later on the 10th, Lancasters made the first attack for which they were designed, when two of No. 44's aircraft joined a bomber force 126-strong to raid Essen. Each of the Lancasters carried a 5,000-lb load of incendiaries.

Operations for No. 97 Squadron commenced on 20 March 1942 when six Lancasters joined 13 Manchesters to lay mines in waters around the Frisian Islands. The poor weather upon their return forced the aircraft to change their routeing with three aircraft landing at airfields in

Right: Aircraft having to ditch did not normally stay afloat too long, but W4318 PM-C of No. 103 Squadron defied all the odds by staying on the surface for 33 hours! Hit by flak on a raid against La Spezia, Italy on the night of 13/14 April 1943, the Lancaster ran out of fuel forcing its skipper, Sergeant John Stoneman, to put it down in the Channel. The crew was successfully rescued from their dinghy by a combination of a Supermarine Walrus and an RAF launch after just over three hours. An attempt was made to tow the aircraft the 50 miles to Falmouth, but the salvage vessel collided with the Lancaster's tail, causing the machine to sink.

Oxfordshire and two eventually finding their base at Coningsby. The bad visibility caused the loss of one of the Lancasters as, after hitting the roof of a house with the trailing aerial, the aircraft crash-landed on the beach at Freiston, Lincolnshire, without injury to the crew members. However, the machine was then swamped by the tide and had to be written-off.

The first loss of a Lancaster crew on an operational sortie came on the night of 24/25 March 1942 when a No. 44 Squadron aircraft failed to return from minelaying near Lorient, France. The Lancaster was lost without trace and is believed to have been damaged by flak while in the target area and presumably crashed into the sea.

Slowly but surely the build-up of Lancasters was gathering momentum as on the following night Nos 44 and 97 Squadrons despatched seven Lancasters to join 247 aircraft in an attack on the Krupps facilities at Essen. No Lancasters were lost.

The first Lancaster to be lost by No. 207 Squadron was in a collision with a Miles Master

aircraft during a training flight on 28 March 1942. The four crew members on board the bomber died when the aircraft crashed at Canwick Hill near Lincoln. The pilot in the Master was also killed.

During March a total of 54 Lancasters had been delivered to the three squadrons, but it was the first two units which had received instructions to carry out long-distance formation flights particularly up to Scotland. These flights were undertaken by the most experienced crews while newcomers to the squadrons were to take over minelaying and some bombing operations.

It was obvious that a special operation was being planned as the intense low-level training continued with both squadrons joining forces for an exercise on 14 April 1942. Aircraft from No. 44 Squadron would be under the command of Squadron Leader John Nettleton while Squadron Leader John Sherwood would lead No. 97 Squadron. On the morning of 17 April 1942, the special target was revealed as the MAN factory at Augsburg in southern Germany which manufactured diesel engines for U-boats and a

Hauptman Heinz Schweizer of the Luftwaffe describes the bomb from Flight Lieutenant Barlow's Lancaster ED917 AJ-E, which had crashed with the loss of the crew after hitting high tension wires during the Dams attack. The bomb was recovered intact as the photograph, taken on 17 May 1943 shows, and just nine days later the German bomb disposal units had complete diagrams of the weapon. In addition, the Luftwaffe had been furnished with drawings of the delivery method gleaned from the wreckage of other crashed Lancasters.

Below: The price of war. All that remains of a Lancaster's rear fuselage and tail unit is shown in this German photograph taken after a raid on Hamburg.

Above: Engine runs for ED759 UV-X of No. 460 (RAAF) Squadron at Breighton early in May 1943. This unit was the first of three Australian squadrons to be equipped with the Lancaster, receiving its first aircraft in October 1942. The Squadron's code letters changed from UV to AR later in May, but ED759 would not wear them for long as it was shot down on the raid to Wuppertal during the night of 29th/30th of that month.

Right: Armourers loading 1,000-lb bombs into a Lancaster in 1943. The aircraft had completed 46 operations at the time of the photograph and, although the individual letter is the same, it is not the famous 'S for Sugar', R5868, which now resides in the RAF Museum at Hendon.

variety of munitions. There would be six aircraft from each unit with Nettleton leading. The route took the force over the Channel, continuing down the French coast before turning east towards the Swiss border. The aircraft then headed toward Munich before changing course for Augsburg. It was hoped that attacks in northern France by RAF Bostons and aircraft of Fighter Command would distract the Germans from the bombers, but this failed as four of the Lancasters were shot down en route. Eight aircraft reached the target to bomb accurately, but the heavily defended area around the factory boasted a large variety of gun types and these were able to destroy three more of the attacking force including the Lancaster of John Sherwood who, amazingly, survived the crash of his aircraft while the rest of his crew were killed. The five remaining bombers headed home across France fully expecting to be attacked by Luftwaffe fighters, but none came. Nettleton's was the only aircraft of No. 44 Squadron to survive, while of the four Lancasters remaining from No. 97, one of them was declared a write-off on the following day. The reconnaissance photographs showed extensive damage in the target area, delighting both Churchill and the Admiralty. John Nettleton was awarded the Victoria Cross for his leadership, but because of the heavy losses in experienced crews and aircraft the raid

Wings for Victory Week in July 1943 took place in a number of cities, but it was ED749 in Piccadilly, Manchester, which gave the author his first chance to see a complete Lancaster. The brand-new aircraft had been transported from Woodford for the event and after service with Nos 100 and 300 Squadrons, followed by a period at No. 1 Lancaster Finishing School (LFS), the aircraft did survive the war. Another of the exhibits was the fuselage of a Lancaster which was unskinned in sections to show the aircraft's internal structure and fittings.

was never repeated. Nettleton was to lose his life later in the war when his Lancaster was shot down by German night fighters returning from a raid on Turin on 12/13 July 1943.

Just ten days after Augsburg Nos 44 and 97 Squadrons were on call again, this time to send 12 Lancasters to join 31 Halifaxes in an attack on the German battleship *Tirpitz* which was anchored near Trondheim, Norway. The bombing was poor however, and no damage was done to the vessel. The raid was made at a cost of four Halifaxes and one of No. 97's aircraft which was hit by flak and crashed in the target area with the loss of the crew.

The arrival of Lancasters in No. 5 Group was continuing steadily with No. 83 Squadron and No. 106 Squadron both receiving aircraft during

April 1942. The latter was under the command of Wing Commander Guy Penrose Gibson who, of course, would add to the Lancaster's proud record just over one year later.

The night of 30/31 May 1942 is famous for the first of the so-called '1,000 Bomber Raids' – on Cologne – the Lancaster squadrons contributing 73 aircraft to the total force. The latest unit to receive the Lancaster, No. 50 Squadron at Skellingthorpe, did not want to miss out on this historic attack with its new charge and provided a single aircraft. Only one Lancaster was lost, but

In one of the best ever Lancaster photographs, Mk II DS723 EQ-B of No. 408 Squadron lifts off at Linton-on-Ouse in August 1943. This Canadian squadron's commanding officer, Wing Commander A.C. Mair, was at the controls of DS723 when it was lost without trace during an attack on Berlin on 26/27 November 1943. The bulged bomb doors are well illustrated.

The air and ground crew of W4783 G-George, AR-G of No. 460 (RAAF) Squadron, pose with the aircraft after completing 70 operations in November 1943. The aircraft was subsequently presented to Australia, departing from Binbrook on 6 October 1944 after a reported 90 operations. Flown in Australia as A66-2, the Lancaster is now displayed at the War Museum in Canberra, painted in its wartime colours.

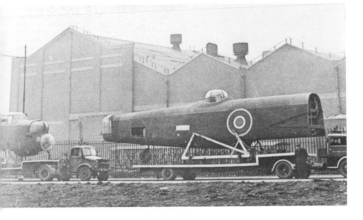

this too was from one of the new units, No. 61 Squadron at Syerston.

Throughout the summer and autumn of 1942 Lancasters were increasingly involved in Bomber Command's attacks, with occasional detachments for coastal patrol and anti-shipping duties, during which a No. 61 Squadron aircraft sank the German submarine *U-571* on 17 July.

One of the Metropolitan-Vickers-built Lancasters leaves the Trafford Park factory on low-loaders for its journey to the Woodford assembly line. Metro-Vick manufactured 1,080 Lancasters, but there is no clue to the identity of this example as the serial numbers were taped over for security reasons.

Right: German civilians inspect the wreckage of ND408, PM-T of No. 103 Squadron, which crashed nine miles south of Paderborn after the raid on Leipzig on 19/20 February 1944.

An important daylight attack on 17 October 1942 saw No. 5 Group using nine squadrons of Lancasters adding Nos 9, 49 and 57 to those used in previous actions. The raid, codename Operation *Robinson* was against the massive Schneider armaments factory at Le Creusot, France, and was led by Wing Commander L.C. Slee of No. 49 Squadron. The low-level route took the force over 300 miles across France with 88 aircraft attacking the main target while six others were to bomb a transformer station at

Left: Heavy snow in the early months of 1944 made operations difficult for all involved as this photograph, taken at Waddington, proves. The aircraft in the picture, ED606 JO-E of No. 463 (RAAF) Squadron, collided with ND637 CF-L of No. 625 Squadron while returning from Stuttgart in the morning of 16 March 1944. Both Lancasters crashed at Branston, Lincolnshire with the loss of their crews.

nearby Montchanin which provided electric power for the main factory. The raid took the Germans completely by surprise as the targets were bombed with the loss of only a Lancaster of No. 61 Squadron from the small force which attacked the transformer building. Six of its crew were killed, with the lone survivor being made a

A peaceful scene at Skellingthorpe on 10 May 1944 as ND991 VN-P of No. 50 Squadron awaits its first operation that evening, when it went to railway yards at Lille. Amazingly, the aircraft had made its maiden flight only ten days before, when Ken Cook cleared it for immediate delivery. After only two operations it was loaned to Flight Refuelling Limited for trials work before returning to service as GN-H of the Bombing Development Unit. The aircraft was sold for scrap on 21 August 1949.

Photographs of aircraft equipped with 'Airborne Cigar' (ABC) are rare and although this particular shot is well known it does serve as an excellent illustration of the Lancaster's large aerials. The security surrounding the installation was tight and this picture was taken from inside the doorway of a dispersal hut! The aircraft was LL757 SR-W of No. 101 Squadron at Ludford Magna in May 1944. Unfortunately the machine was lost three months later when it crashed in Sweden returning from Stettin on 29/30 August 1944, with its eight-man crew being killed.

prisoner of war. During the raid, one of No. 207's aircraft turned back because of engine trouble, but was attacked by three Arado Ar 196 seaplanes. This turned out to be a mistake for the Germans as two of the opposition were shot down by the Lancaster's gunners while the third gave up the attack. Sadly, the bomber's flight engineer was killed in this action.

In the latter months of 1942 Bomber Command set its sights on targets in Italy, paying particular attention to Turin, Milan and Genoa, but was also able to launch attacks against Hamburg, Stuttgart, Mannheim, Duisburg and Munich, with minelaying sorties also still on the agenda.

The beginning of 1943 saw a number of smaller raids, but on the night of 16/17 January Bomber Command visited the 'Big City', Berlin, for the first time in over a year with a force of 201 aircraft comprising 190 Lancasters and 11 Halifaxes. As the Luftwaffe's early warning system did not work the losses were unexpectedly light, with only a No. 61 Squadron Lancaster and its crew being lost. The raid was repeated the following night with 170 Lancasters and 17 Halifaxes, however, this time 19 Lancasters and three Halifaxes failed to return.

As the war progressed, extensive developments in navigation and blind-bombing aids gave the

bombers a higher level of accuracy with the first of these systems being known as 'Gee'. In 1943 the use of the 'Gee' radio beam navigation system continued, but the introduction of the 'Oboe' blind-bombing device proved to be a boon for Bomber Command. This system, which had been used on a number of operations in 1942, incorporated radar-ranging from two ground stations on the English coast. These transmitted signals to the bomber, which were then retransmitted to the stations, with the elapsed time used to calculate the aircraft's exact position. A short signal was then transmitted to initiate the bomb release. It was realised that 'Oboe's' best use could be as a guide for Pathfinder aircraft, but the limited range of the system meant that a number of areas in Germany could be free from that kind of attack.

The Pathfinder Force had been established on 15 August 1942 under Group Captain Donald Bennett and the effectiveness of this unit was already evident. It also employed other improved techniques for marking targets more accurately. These included Target Indicators in the shape of bomb casings packed with pyrotechnics and equipped with barometric fuses which could be set to release the 'fireworks' at a required altitude. These markers fell like a large bunch of grapes in selected glowing colours over the aiming point. The introduction of the ground-scanning H_2S radar system into Bomber Command aircraft was another boost. The operator was presented with a radar picture of the ground below, on which he could pick out coastlines, rivers and towns. In the early stages the outlines of buildings were poorly represented, but the device was continually improved as the war progressed. In the electronic battle, British and German scientists introduced measures and counter-measures throughout the war with ingenious devices being produced by both sets of 'boffins'. Codenames including 'Rebecca', 'Monica', 'Tinsel', 'Window' and a host of others became part of the RAF's vocabulary.

The Battle of the Ruhr

The attack on Essen on the night of 5/6 March 1943 signified the start of an intensive bombing campaign known as the Battle of the Ruhr. Sustained raids upon industrial targets including Bochum, Dortmund, Duisburg, Düsseldorf, Essen and Mülheim became commonplace while the cities of Berlin, Nuremburg, Stuttgart and Munich also received their share of attention. The bombing of Essen at the start of the Battle saw 157 Lancasters joining a total force of 442 aircraft including eight de Havilland Mosquitos which led the attack using the 'Oboe' blind-bombing system. The raid caused much damage to the Krupps factory and devastated a large area of the city.

The massive build-up of Lancaster production meant that in less than one year since the first

operations, the increased deliveries now saw ten squadrons in No. 5 Group, five in No. 1 Group, one squadron in No. 3 Group plus two squadrons in No. 8 (PFF) Group, all equipped with the Lancaster. By the war's end Bomber Command would have 57 Lancaster squadrons including ten in the Canadian No. 6 Group and eight in the PFF Group.

Operation *Chastise*

The RAF Station at Scampton was just another operational bomber base until the middle of May 1943 when it became known as probably the most famous of the wartime bomber airfields. However, before that historic time Scampton was certainly in the news as, on 15 March 1943, a bomb fell from a No. 57 Squadron Lancaster while the aircraft was being loaded. The bomb detonated with such force that the blast destroyed five more Lancasters parked in the vicinity with two others being from the same unit while the other three belonged to No. 50 Squadron. Amazingly, there were no casualties.

The most publicised bombing raid of World War Two was launched from Scampton just two months after the disastrous explosion. In a move unprecedented in RAF history, a squadron was formed to undertake a special operation. This unit, No. 617 Squadron, was formed at Scampton on 21 March 1943 under the command of Wing Commander Guy Gibson specifically to breach the great Ruhr dams of the Möhne, Eder and Sorpe which contained over 300 million tons of water vital to the industrial centres of Germany. Gibson, an outstanding bomber pilot, was allowed the privilege of selecting the crews for this operation, but was unaware of the task the unit was to perform.

A Lancaster on the wrong end of an Allied attack is seen in this shot taken from the camera gun of an 8th Air Force North American P-51 Mustang strafing a German airfield in late 1944. It is known that ND396 BQ-D of No. 550 Squadron, which crash-landed near Berlin on 30/31 January 1944, was repaired and evaluated by the Luftwaffe. However, that aircraft was flown in its normal camouflage, but with yellow engine nacelles and wing tips and German markings. The aircraft in the photograph appears to be intact, with an RAF roundel visible on the port wing, the starboard wing marking being obscured by bullet strikes. The identity of a second Lancaster remains a mystery.

A Lancaster of No. 103 Squadron is seen attacking targets in the Pas de Calais area in July 1944. The light coloured streaks on the wings were caused by the exhaust gases from the leaded fuel.

This attack, codenamed *Chastise*, was to be carried out by the Squadron using Lancasters, modified under the guidance of Avro's Roy Chadwick, to be armed with a special mine designed by Dr Barnes Wallis of Vickers-Armstrong at Weybridge. More commonly known as the 'bouncing bomb', the weapon had to be released at 60 ft at a speed of exactly 220 mph to obtain results. The entire operation was to be flown at low level to avoid detection.

On the night of 16/17 May 1943, Gibson led the 19 aircraft to attack in three waves. As the raid progressed one aircraft had to return to Scampton after hitting the sea, a collision which tore the mine from its mounts. Another was forced to return after flak damaged the radio causing a complete loss of communications, but sadly, eight aircraft were lost during the operation. Five of the bombers were either shot down or crashed before reaching the target area, leaving 12 Lancasters to complete the bombing. Gibson's and four other aircraft bombed and breached the Möhne dam, while three others breached the Eder. Others

attacked the Sorpe and Schwelme dams without success and one other failed to find any of the targets, returning to base without releasing the mine. Three of the Lancasters were lost after bombing the dams. The loss of the water caused great disruption to German industry through widespread flooding and reconnaissance photographs clearly showed the breached dams and the extent of that flooding. For showing great courage and determination in pressing home this attack Gibson was awarded the Victoria Cross, with 34 of his men receiving various decorations. The cost in experienced bomber crews was high, with 53 airmen being killed and three becoming prisoners of war, but the damage caused to the German war effort was enormous, the *Goebbels Diaries* for 18 May 1943 quotes, 'Air Raids during the night inflicted heavy damage to us. The attacks of British bombers on the dams in our valleys were very successful. The Führer is exceedingly impatient and angry about the lack of preparedness on the part of the Luftwaffe. Damage to production was more than normal. Naturally the Gauleiters in areas containing dams which have not yet been attacked are very much worried, since the anti-aircraft measures there are quite inadequate.'

After a relatively quiet period in Bomber Command operations it was Dortmund which was attacked in the heavy raid of 23/24 May 1943 when a force of 826 aircraft bombed the city, completely destroying the Hoesch steelworks. This attack marked the first time that over 300 Lancasters had been used in a single raid as 343 took part with eight of those failing to return.

Large scale operations in June saw the final phase in the Battle of the Ruhr, although the bombers returned many times to the industrial centre of Germany before the war ended.

After just one operation No. 617 Squadron would be known for ever as the 'Dam Busters' and it was decided by Bomber Command that this unit would be retained as a specialised bombing squadron. The Squadron was brought up to full operational strength in personnel and re-equipped with standard Lancasters.

The reports on the dams attack proved the successful use of a VHF radio by Gibson to control the whole operation. From this experience came the plan for a 'Master Bomber' to control any attack by directing the raid and reporting its accuracy. To put this idea into operation a force of 60 Lancasters took part in a significant raid on the old Zeppelin factory at Friedrichshafen on 20/21 June 1943. The target, on the northern shore of Lake Constance on the German-Swiss border, was engaged in the production of the *Würzburg* radar equipment so vital to the Luftwaffe's fighter defences. The operation, codenamed *Bellicose,* included 56 bombers from No. 5 Group plus four of No. 8 Group's PFF aircraft. The Pathfinders of No. 97 Squadron were led by the 'Controller', Group Captain Leonard Slee, however, his aircraft developed engine trouble and, reluctantly, he had to hand over the task to his deputy, Wing Commander Cosmo Gomm of No. 467 Squadron. The attack was to be carried out at a relatively low level, an altitude of 11,000 ft was

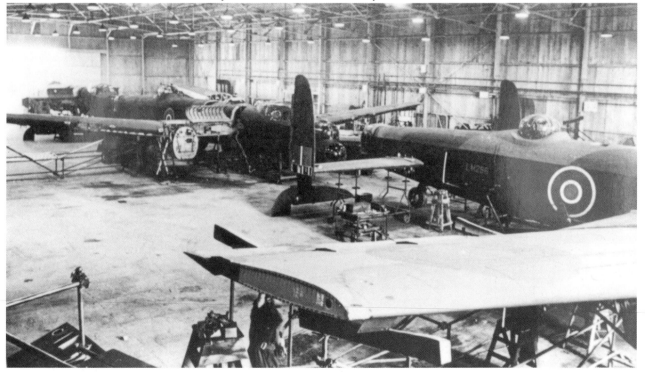

The Armstrong Whitworth production hangar at Bittesewell shows LM296 followed by what appears to be an Avro Manchester, but it is a Lancaster awaiting the two outboard engines! The former became VN-T of No. 50 Squadron and after being badly damaged on 16 November 1944 while attacking Düren in support of the US Army, it went on to complete a total of 54 operations before the war's end.

planned en route, but on arrival at the target the intense anti-aircraft fire convinced Gomm that the raid should be made from 16,000 ft. The PFF marking was not as accurate as expected, but using the 'Master Bomber' technique to perfection, Gomm was able to direct proceedings causing serious damage to the factory. Just 29 years earlier Avro bombers had also raided the Zeppelin factory, but these were Avro 504s of the Royal Naval Air Service.

The Luftwaffe was taken completely by surprise on the outward leg of the attack, but massed to intercept the raiders on their way home, however, it was fooled again as the Lancasters flew on to Maison Blanche and Blida in Algeria without loss. Three nights after the attack on Friedrichshafen the bombers left their North African base, attacking an arms dump and oil storage depot at La Spezia, Italy on the return to England. Once again the Germans were taken by surprise and no aircraft were lost.

The Italian city of Turin was the main target for the night of 12/13 July 1943 when 295 Lancasters of Nos 1, 5 and 8 Groups made the attack. Of the 14 aircraft lost was the Lancaster piloted by Wing Commander John Nettleton, who had been awarded the Victoria Cross for the attack on Augsburg on 17 April 1942. His Lancaster was shot down by a German night fighter into the sea off Brest on the return flight from the target. One particularly sad loss was that of a No. 467 Squadron aircraft which, although heavily damaged, was able to return to its base at Bottesford only to break up on the approach to the airfield killing all on board.

The Battle of Hamburg

Bomber Command entered a new phase of operations commencing 24/25 July 1943 with a number of heavy raids on Hamburg. With the development of the radio and radar aids installed in the heavy bombers, the German port was an ideal target to show the full potential of H_2S as every PFF aircraft was now equipped with the system. Hamburg was out of the range of 'Oboe', but the distinctly shaped shoreline around the city would be well displayed on the H_2S operator's screen. The operation to start what became known as the Battle of Hamburg, saw a bomber force of 791 aircraft, including 347 Lancasters, use 'Window' for the first time. 'Window' consisted of a strip of black paper with aluminium on one side which, when released in quantity, caused complete confusion amongst the German defences with ground radars, radar-controlled flak guns and night fighters all

Air and ground crew proudly pose with their new aircraft, PB880, which was their present for Christmas 1944. Becoming LE-B of No. 630 Squadron, the machine was only just one month old when it was scheduled to join another 217 No. 5 Group Lancasters to attack oil targets at Pölitz. While en route to the target the starboard outer engine caught fire and refused to be extinguished forcing the crew to bale out as the captain headed for Sweden, where the aircraft crashed on 13 January 1945.

Seen over the snow-covered countryside in January 1945, NG361 of No. 149 Squadron completed a number of operations before hostilities ceased. The aircraft stayed with the Squadron at Methwold until 23 April 1946 when it was put into storage with No. 10 Maintenance Unit (MU) at Hullavington until Struck off Charge (SOC) on 27 February 1947.

receiving false echoes. This confusion meant that out of the attacking force only 12 aircraft, four of them Lancasters, were lost.

The raids on Hamburg are remembered for the massive firestorm which devastated the city in the attack of 27/28 July. This was due to a number of factors, but mainly the freak weather conditions which had seen temperatures of over 30°C with low humidity and a lack of rain for over two months. The various fires then joined together into one massive inferno with the air being forced into it by storm force winds. The firestorm continued for over three hours consuming everything in its path which, besides the great loss of life, provided the German High Command with the task of feeding and housing over one million homeless people. On this operation 11 Lancasters were lost out of the attacking force of 787 aircraft with 353 of these being the Avro bomber.

The Battle of Hamburg ended sooner than expected with the last of the four heavy bomber raids taking place on the night of 2/3 August 1943. Hamburg would be visited again by Bomber Command before the end of the war, but never with such intensity.

Striking Peenemünde

Intelligence reports reaching London, mainly from Denmark and Norway, told of the increasing number of developments by the Germans including a variety of missiles and long-range rockets. The existence of Peenemünde on the Baltic coast was already known to the Allies, but the lack of information on the exact nature of the work being undertaken was frustrating for the intelligence services. It was in June 1943 that aerial reconnaissance photographs showed two objects which were thought to be rockets, but this theory was dismissed by Professor Lindeman, Chief Scientific Adviser to the Government, who claimed the objects were nothing more than huge barrage balloons! However, confirmation of the large rocket development came from a Luxemburger, working as forced labour at Peenemünde, who reported that these long-range weapons were to be used against Britain. Plans were immediately made to undertake a large-scale raid against the site, although there would be some delay until the bombers could make the long flight and arrive over the target in darkness. The night selected was 17/18 August 1943 when 595 aircraft, including 324 Lancasters, were despatched to destroy the German research establishment. A diversionary raid was made against Berlin by eight Mosquitos of No. 139 Squadron which, it was hoped, would divert Luftwaffe night fighters from the main attack. The 'Master Bomber' for this attack was Group Captain John Searby of No. 83 Squadron who controlled the bombers throughout the operation and it was estimated that the rocket programme, later to be confirmed as the V-2, was put back at

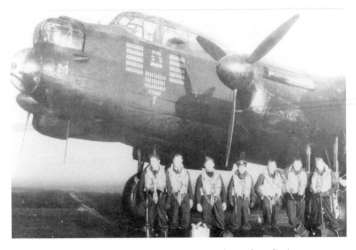

'Mike Squared', or ED888, made its first flight on 15 April 1943 in the hands of Jimmy Orrell and by the 20th of that month it was at Elsham Wolds joining No. 103 Squadron as PM-M. After 32 operations the aircraft was transferred to the newly formed No. 576 Squadron, on the same station as UL-V². On 21 March 1944, four months after going to the new squadron, the aircraft's individual letter was again changed to 'M-Mike' as UL-M². The Lancaster's operations steadily mounted, the aircraft completing its 100th on 20 July 1944. On 31 October 1944, ED888 went back to No. 103 Squadron as PM-M² and besides 'Mike Squared' it was also known as 'The Mother of them All'. This photograph shows Flight Lieutenant S.L. Saxe, RCAF, and his crew after returning from the aircraft's last operation, which was to Cologne on Christmas Eve 1944. A total of 140 operations were flown, but there was no sentiment as ED888 was sold for scrap on 8 January 1947.

least three months. Sadly, some of the bombs fell onto the barracks of the forced labour unit, probably killing the brave Luxemburger, as he was never heard from again. The faint attack on Berlin did work for a time, but the Luftwaffe arrived in numbers before the raid was completed and it was the bombers in the last wave which came in for severe punishment. The night fighters used their upwards-firing guns, codenamed *Schräge Musik* for the first time with some success as Bomber Command lost 15 Halifaxes, two Stirlings and 23 Lancasters. One Mosquito was lost from the diversion while another was badly damaged in a crash-landing on return to base.

Sir Arthur Harris, Head of Bomber Command, was confident that the aircraft could now range deep into Germany, and find, mark and bomb any target. By the end of August 1943 raids against Berlin had been launched with the opening attack being on the night of the 23rd, followed on 31 August/1 September and 3/4 September. These raids were classed as 'dress rehearsals', but still cost 125 bombers including 49 Lancasters, with the last of these attacks being carried out by 316 of the Avro bomber, and four Mosquitos, the latter being detailed to drop marker flares well away from the heavy bombers' route to distract the night fighters. The all-Lancaster bombing force was despatched because of the heavy losses sustained by the Stirlings and Halifaxes on the previous Berlin operations. On this attack 22 Lancasters failed to return. It was during this period that 'Corona' became operational. 'Corona' involved voice deception carried out by German-speaking men and women broadcasting false information to the Luftwaffe's night fighters. The confused pilots would not know which controller was giving them the correct instructions as both voices would claim to be the 'real' one. Lancasters of No. 101 Squadron were equipped with ABC, codenamed 'Airborne Cigar', which was first used in an attack on Stuttgart on 7/8 October 1943. This device was used to jam enemy radio frequencies and a

This extremely interesting photograph shows PB457 'V-Victor' of No. 101 Squadron awaiting repair after receiving damage on the Nuremberg raid of 2/3 January 1945. An ABC-equipped aircraft shown with its aerials removed, 'V-Victor' suffered further damage while repairs were underway when on 3 February 1945, it caught fire in one of Ludford Magna's hangars and was completely destroyed. Its replacement, PA237 SR-V, was shot down over Pforzheim on 23/24th of that month.

German-speaking radio operator was carried as an extra crew member with the task, similar to that of the ground-based 'Corona' operators, of confusing the Luftwaffe fighters. The aircraft carried a normal bomb load, less the weight of the ABC equipment and the operator.

The heavy raids continued against a number of German cities with Berlin being the main target. However, on the night of 14/15 September 1943, No. 617 Squadron, now under the command of Squadron Leader George Holden, would once again be called upon to perform a special operation. The Squadron's task would be to attack the Dortmund-Ems canal using the new 12,000-lb High Capacity (HC) bombs, the unit's Lancasters having the associated bulged bomb-doors modification. The target was one of Germany's main supply routes between the industrial Ruhr and the ports, as it was used to ship coal and raw material to the factories while, in the other direction, components for the German shipyards were also transported. The defences surrounding the canal had taken a heavy toll of Bomber Command aircraft on previous visits, with the attackers failing to cause any serious damage. The main area for the raid was Ladbergen, north-east of Munster, as the low-lying countryside in the vicinity was below the level of the canal and any breach would empty a large distance of the waterway while also flooding the immediate area. Eight

Lancasters took off from their new home at Coningsby, but while the force was crossing the North Sea one of the weather reconnaissance Mosquitos radioed that the whole of the target area was blanketed by thick fog. An immediate recall message was issued and the Lancasters turned back, but as they did so Squadron Leader D.J.H. Maltby's aircraft crashed into the sea off Cromer, Norfolk, with the loss of the crew. With the weapons still on board the aircraft, excess fuel had to be jettisoned for the Lancasters to reach a safe landing weight. The initial briefing had instructed the crews to retain the bomb if the attack was aborted for any reason.

On the following evening eight aircraft were again despatched to attack the canal with Flight Lieutenant H.B. 'Micky' Martin taking the place of Maltby. Clear weather had been reported at Ladbergen, but when the Lancasters arrived the mist had descended once more with only small breaks to show short stretches of the waterway. Flying at 100 ft the bombers met heavy anti-aircraft fire with five aircraft being lost including that of the Commanding Officer, George Holden. Casualties, including those of the previous night, totalled 48 with 20 of those being survivors of the Dams attack, confirming that low-level raids against heavily defended targets was too great a price to pay especially as the Dortmund-Ems canal raid was a total failure with no breaches of the banks being achieved. A personnel

On 4 August 1944 thirteen Lancasters made their first test flight from Woodford, with PB410 having the honour of being flown by Avro chief test pilot Sam Brown. Having come through the war unscathed with No. 97 Squadron, the aircraft was passed to No. 12 Squadron in 1946. The subsequent arrival of the Avro Lincoln spelt the end for No. 12's Lancasters and PB410 was placed on the scrap heap in January 1947.

Lancasters of No. 5 Group en route to bomb railway bridges near Bremen on 22 March 1945. The aircraft in the centre of the photograph is ME329 JO-A of No. 463 (RAAF) Squadron, while to the rear of centre is PO-S, R5868 of No. 467 (RAAF), Squadron, which now has a place of honour in the RAF Museum at Hendon.

replacement programme for the missing crews was initiated and No. 617 Squadron started to be retrained as a high-altitude bombing unit. The Squadron's Lancasters were equipped with the new Stabilised Automatic Bomb sight (SABS) which would, being gyro-stabilised, enable the bomb aimer to compute the release point with the SABS transmitting information to the pilot for any changes in heading before the bombs were automatically released at the correct point. On 11 November 1943 the Squadron received a new CO, Wing Commander Leonard Cheshire. The weather was a constant problem for the

bomber crews who were normally returning from raids well into the early hours of the morning just as the mist was rising over many of the bases. The sea fog too was a great hazard and it will never be known just how many aircraft were lost by flying into the North Sea or the Channel. In November 1943 the first of 15 selected airfields was equipped with the Fog Investigation and Dispersal Operation (FIDO) system which involved the burning of fuel piped along the side of a main runway with the flames dispersing the fog and also providing the pilot with a visual landing aid while approaching in

Yeadon built Mk I ME432 of No. 467 (RAAF) Squadron, was delivered to the unit on 3 January 1945 and had a comparatively easy war. On 3/4 March it carried out its first operation by going to Ladbergen where it was so badly damaged that repairs lasted until the end of the war. It was later flown by Nos 635 and 35 Squadrons before it became surplus and was sold for scrap in October 1946.

Loading bombs was a specialised operation, but the ten-ton 'Grand Slam' was exceptional as it did not fit completely into the aircraft and required a large attachment strap to keep it in place. This Lancaster B.Mk I (Special) PD119, YZ-J of No. 617 Squadron, is being loaded at Woodhall Spa in March 1945.

poor weather. This system proved to be one of the great success stories of the war as almost 2,500 aircraft were recovered by these means before the end of hostilities.

Before the period which became known as the Battle of Berlin started, a raid on Düsseldorf on the night of 3/4 November 1943 saw a force of 589 aircraft attack the city. The raid was notable in that 38 radial-engined Lancaster Mk IIs taken from Nos 3 and 6 Groups had joined the Main Force equipped for the first time with the G-H blind-bombing system to attack the giant Mannesmann steel plant. However, through operational difficulties only 15 of the aircraft actually bombed using the device, albeit with excellent results. The operational plan called for a diversionary raid on Cologne with 52 of the 344 Lancasters in the Main Force breaking away to carry out this attack. In this raid no aircraft were lost, but the Düsseldorf attack cost 18 aircraft with 11 of those being Lancasters. It was during the main attack that Flight Lieutenant William Reid of No. 61 Squadron was severely wounded by a night fighter en route to the target, while a second attack killed his navigator and radio operator. Reid was also wounded in this second attack, but decided to go on to the target as to turn back into the bomber stream would have meant a certain collision. After dropping its bombs the Lancaster headed for home with the aircraft's flight engineer, who was also wounded, giving his captain oxygen. Even with his wounds, a shattered windscreen and a heavily damaged aircraft to contend with, Reid

guided the Lancaster back to England to make a perfect crash-landing at the USAAF base at Shipdham in Norfolk. William Reid was awarded the country's highest honour – the Victoria Cross. Reid's flight engineer was awarded the Conspicuous Gallantry Medal (CGM), while the rear gunner received a DFC.

The Battle of Berlin

The opening assault in the period known as the Battle of Berlin came on the night of 18/19 November 1943 when an all-Lancaster bombing force of 440, supplemented by four Mosquitos, attacked the city. Simultaneously, a force of Halifaxes and Stirlings with 24 PFF Lancasters was sent to raid Mannheim. Cloud cover over Berlin kept fighter attacks down, but flak continued to be heavy, claiming nine Lancasters. The Mannheim operation lost 23 of the bombing force, including two Lancasters. A few attacks later, on 26/27 November, the raiders lost 28 Lancasters during the assault, but disastrously lost 14 more in crashes in England due to poor weather conditions. It was a similar situation after the raid on Berlin on 16/17 December 1943 when an incredible 29 Lancasters were destroyed on return to their bases in addition to the 25 lost during the attack.

In the four months from 18 November 1943 until 31 March 1944 the 'Big City' was attacked 16 times by Bomber Command while other large cities also received their share of attention. In addition, the confirmation of the existence of a small pilotless aircraft being developed by the

It is hard to believe that this aircraft flew all the way from Dortmund to make an emergency landing at Manston with such severe flak damage. No. 156 Squadron's ME378 'Q-Queenie' was bracketed by flak while approaching the large Benzol plant at Harpenerweg. After ordering the crew to abandon the aircraft, the captain regained control and flew the Lancaster back to England minus three crew members who had baled out. It is also hard to believe that, at such a late period in the war with surplus Lancasters available, the aircraft was repaired and put into storage until it was sold for scrap in March 1948.

Luftwaffe as a flying-bomb – known as the V-1 – and reconnaissance photographs showing ramp-like structures located in coastal areas of France and pointing in the direction of London, required action by Bomber Command during December 1943. Another attack during 'the Battle' period was the highly successful bombing of the Gnome-Rhône aero engine plant at Limoges in France by 12 Lancasters of No. 617 Squadron led by Wing Commander Leonard Cheshire. Cheshire requested that he mark the

target at low level and after making three runs over the factory to allow the workers to take cover, the fourth run dropped incendiaries at less the 100 ft altitude, marking the aiming point accurately. The remaining 11 Lancasters unloaded their 12,000-lb bombs with similar accuracy, completely destroying the factory.

As prelude to the invasion at Normandy, Sir Arthur Harris had to direct his bombers away from their main attacks on Germany to the planning of precision targets on the French coast in support of the ground forces. The last great raid before the start of that period was on the night 30/31 March 1944, when a large force of bombers attacked Nuremburg. However, the raid was a disaster as, because of extremely poor weather over the target area, the PFF's marking

No. 419 (RCAF) Squadron Lancasters line up for the mission to Wangerooge, in the Frisian Islands, on 25 April 1945, with the crews not knowing that it would be No. 6 Group's last operation. The main aircraft in the picture was KB999 VR-M *Malton Mike*, named as a tribute to the factory which built it. The 300th Mk X, it returned to Canada on 28 June 1945 and after conversion to Mk 10MR standard served with No. 405 Squadron, RCAF. It was destroyed in a crash on 22 October 1953.

Frank Chambers, skipper of PB782 EM-Y of No. 207 Squadron, his air and ground crew, celebrate VE-Day, the end of the war in Europe, in the sunshine at Spilsby. Test pilot Reg Knight had made the aircraft's first flight on 10 November 1944, with the machine joining No. 207 on the 23rd of that month. Exactly a year to the day of its maiden flight, 10 November 1945, PB782 was declared surplus by the RAF.

was hampered by high winds and little damage was done. This operation cost the greatest losses suffered by Bomber Command during the war as the German defences were thought to have been alerted by the crew of a PFF Mosquito who inadvertently broadcast a discussion between the pilot and his navigator on the planning of the attack. At the de-briefing, a number of the Mosquito crews reported having heard the conversation and, presumably, so did the Germans. Whatever the cause, the Command lost 11.9 per cent of the 795 bombers despatched, including 64 Lancasters and 31 Halifaxes.

The tactical bombing of targets in France and Belgium proved to be highly successful as, besides being important areas, these raids were also part of a deception plan to persuade the enemy into thinking that any landings would be made in the Pas de Calais area. The attacks would be headed by the highly experienced Master Bomber crews and despite an occasional

visit to German cities, the units were happy to have the respite that the attacks on tactical targets was able to give them.

On 3/4 May 1944 incredible losses were suffered once again, when 42 Lancasters in an attacking force of 346 failed to return from a raid on the French village of Mailly-le-Camp. A radio failure in the aircraft of the 'Main Force Controller' delayed the attack, allowing Luftwaffe fighters to arrive in numbers. The raid, on a large German army base, was reported to be a success with large-scale destruction of barracks, tanks and motor vehicles. In addition, heavy casualties were suffered among the Wehrmacht troops.

As D-Day dawned on 6 June 1944, Lancasters were already attacking a number of key targets before the assault force arrived on the beaches, while specialised units including No. 617 Squadron dropped large amounts of 'Window' in a number of areas. These aluminium foil strips

Photographed at Witchford on 29 April 1945, this No. 115 Squadron aircraft practises food drops for Operation *Manna*, the delivery of food to starving people in Western Holland. The German area commander arranged a truce for the delivery by Lancasters and 8th Air Force Boeing B-17 Flying Fortresses. The RAF dropped 6,672 tons of food during the operation.

served to confuse the German radar stations into believing that another large invasion fleet was crossing the Channel to a point between Boulogne and Le Havre, well north of the intended landing area.

The first attack using the new 12,000-lb 'Tallboy' bomb after the invasion was to prevent enemy troop movements to Normandy. This attack took place on 8/9 June 1944 against a railway tunnel deep within a hill at Saumur as it was the expected route for the movement of a complete Panzer division from southern France to stiffen resistance against the Allied armies. The bomb, designed for deep penetration, was also the work of Dr Barnes Wallis of Dams fame. Flying a Mosquito, Leonard Cheshire perfectly marked one end of the tunnel while two others completed a similar task at the opposite end. Four Lancasters of No. 83 Squadron then illuminated the area for 25 aircraft of No. 617 Squadron to drop their 'Tallboys' with great accuracy. Reconnaissance photographs taken the following day surprised the Lancaster crews

when they saw the complete devastation caused by the new bomb. One 'Tallboy' had even penetrated the hillside through which the tunnel ran, causing a collapse which had blocked the railway line with thousands of tons of earth.

On 14 June 1944, 221 Lancasters, led by 13 Mosquitos, carried out a daylight attack on the submarine and E-boat pens in the port of Le Havre. The raid was intended to prevent the fast E-boats from harassing the Allied shipping supporting the invasion. The operation was completed in two waves and, in the second wave, 22 aircraft from No. 617 Squadron again carried 'Tallboys'. The bombing was accurate, causing extensive damage to the port area and the concrete-covered pens were hit several times by the 12,000-lb bombs with one even penetrating the 15 ft-thick roof. After this attack the E-boats' aggression disappeared.

Operations in support of the invasion were also supplemented by raids on the V-1 flying-bomb launching sites in France. RAF Bomber Command joined with the 2nd Tactical Air Force and the US 8th Air Force to bomb these targets, significantly reducing the number of these missiles being launched against Britain. The first of these weapons to fall on Britain came down at Swanscombe near Gravesend in the early morning of 13 June 1944.

Sir Arthur Harris still believed that the way to speed the German surrender was to attack the country's cities, causing a full collapse of morale in the German people and he was relieved when Allied Supreme Headquarters returned Bomber Command to the control of the Air Ministry, once again handing over the reins to him. However, it had to be noted that the heavy bombers would again support the troops if the requirement arose. The return came on the night of 16/17 August 1944 when 461 Lancasters attacked the port of Stettin, causing heavy damage and even sinking five ships in the harbour. Five Lancasters were lost.

Germany's giant battleship, *Tirpitz*, posed a constant threat to Allied convoys using the northern supply route to Murmansk in Russia, although the vessel's operations from its Norwegian base had been few. Prime Minister Winston Churchill had ordered that the ship should be a priority target and a number of attacks by aircraft, midget submarines and chariots had caused some damage, but this was repairable. On 15 September 1944 Lancasters of Nos 9 and 617 Squadrons bombed the battleship as it lay at anchor in Kaa Fjord. Twenty of the raiding Lancasters carried 'Tallboys' while seven others delivered 'Johnny Walker' mines designed specifically for launching against ships anchored in shallow water. The Lancasters flew from bases in northern Russia, but a combination of poor weather and a very effective smoke-screen made it impossible to see the ship, with bombs being dropped in the area where the *Tirpitz* was last reported. It was later discovered that one of the 'Tallboys' had hit the battleship's

Flying for fun! Although the threat of fighting the Japanese still hung over many units, the Lancaster crews busied themselves with training flights, the 'Cook's Tours', flights to take the ground crews around the devastated cities of Germany as a 'thank you' for their unsung devotion to duty during the bombing campaign, and any other chance to fly without being shot at! No. 15 Squadron's NG358 shows its yellow G-H tail colours during a flight in May 1945. The aircraft was transferred to the Squadron's C Flight to become DJ-U, before being loaned to Avro for a short period of trials work. It did not escape the axeman however, being Struck off Charge in October 1945.

Photographed at Brussels during Operation *Exodus*, the repatriation of British POWs in May 1945, is PB726 PO-P of No. 467 (RAAF) Squadron. Lancaster squadrons from Nos 1, 5, 6 and 8 Groups performed with great efficiency during the operation, bringing home 74,178 ex-prisoners. PB726 went on to serve with a number of units before it was sold for scrap on 29 August 1947.

bow causing a great amount of damage and allowing 1,500 tons of water to flood into the vessel. In addition, a number of near misses caused varying amounts of damage and, after a thorough investigation by German naval experts, it was decreed that her seagoing days were over. Obviously, the Allies had no knowledge of such a report and the Tirpitz was still a target.

On Hitler's orders the battleship was towed to Tromsø to act as a floating gun battery in the event of an Allied invasion of Norway. This move proved to be a bonus for the Allies as it brought the vessel within striking range of bases in Britain. Once again it was to be the Lancasters of Nos 9 and 617 Squadron, this time fitted with more powerful engines and extra fuel tanks, which were called upon to complete the task. The aircraft left their bases at Bardney and Woodhall Spa on 4 November 1944 to fly up to Lossiemouth in Scotland from where the raid was to be launched. Bad weather delayed the take-off of the overloaded aircraft until 12 November, but it had been vital that the raid take place as soon as possible because of the dwindling daylight hours over Norway. Thirty Lancasters plus a camera aircraft from No. 463 Squadron found the *Tirpitz* in crystal-clear weather and two 'Tallboy' direct hits and a number of near misses caused the vessel to capsize with a heavy loss of life. One Lancaster

was reported missing, but it was later learned that the aircraft had come down in Sweden and the crew was safe.

In 1945 Lancasters were flying an equal amount of daylight operations with both industrial and tactical targets being attacked. The improvement in bombing techniques in the final months of the war required Bomber Command to give priority to oil and transportation targets, but the Harris plan to attack cities continued albeit to a lesser degree. During the final push towards Germany rail targets came in for special treatment with the important viaducts at Arnsburg and Bielefeld being attacked on 14 March 1945. The 12,000-lb 'Tallboy' bombs were dropped by 28 Lancasters, however, it was the giant new 22,000-lb 'Grand Slam' dropped from a No. 617 Squadron aircraft flown by Squadron Leader C.C. Calder which had the greater effect. This, another of Dr Barnes Wallis's creations, created what was described as a 'mini earthquake' which caused more than 100 yards of the Bielefeld viaduct to collapse. The Arnsburg span received similar treatment five days later when five 'Grand Slams' put the viaduct out of action for the remainder of the war and, in fact, for many months afterwards.

The last raids of the war to be made by Bomber Command's Lancasters occurred on 25 April 1945 when 482 aircraft, including 158 of that type, attacked the coastal gun batteries on Wangerooge in the Frisian Islands, sadly with the loss of two aircraft and their crews from No. 431(RCAF) Squadron. In a simultaneous operation 359 Lancasters bombed Hitler's 'Eagle's Nest' and the nearby SS barracks at Berchtesgaden in a highly effective raid. Once again, two Lancasters were lost, but this time 10 of the 14 crew members survived to spend the last few days of the war in captivity. On the night of 25/26 April 1945 107 Lancasters accompanied by 12 Mosquitos successfully bombed the large oil refinery at Tønsberg in Norway. From this attack, No. 463 Squadron had the dubious distinction of having the last Lancaster to be lost on operations. However, after being badly damaged in an attack by a Junkers Ju 88 night fighter, the bomber was able to make its way to neutral Sweden and internment. The end of the war in Europe just a few days later brought an early release.

Operations *Manna* and *Exodus*

Before the surrender was signed, Lancasters were heavily involved in the important task of dropping food to starving Dutch people living in western Holland. Known as Operation *Manna*, these supply operations were potentially

dangerous as large areas were still under German control. However, a truce was arranged with the local Wehrmacht commander and Lancasters from Nos 1, 3 and 8 Groups were able to drop the precious supplies unmolested. The receiving zones were marked by Mosquitos, and 6,672 tons of food were dropped in 2,835 sorties in an operation which is remembered with gratitude to this day. As agreed, there was no enemy action against the Lancasters and the only incident seems to have been with an aircraft of No. 576 Squadron which swung off the runway on take-off, ending in the grass with a collapsed undercarriage. The date was 8 May 1945 and by midnight the war against Germany was over.

The bombing in Europe may have ended, but the Japanese were still to be defeated. However, another important task saw the Lancaster units engaged in Operation *Exodus*, the codename for the repatriation of British prisoners of war recently released from camps in Germany and the occupied countries. As always, the Lancaster squadrons performed with great efficiency, bringing home no fewer than 74,178 ex-prisoners. Sadly, this operation was not completed without loss of life as six crew members of No. 514 Squadron and 24 ex-prisoners, no doubt excited at the prospect of

Lancaster Mk X KB772 served as VR-R with No. 419 (RCAF) Squadron at Middleton St George from 14 November 1944 until the war's end, completing 64 operations. It is interesting that the sharkmouth markings on the cowlings were worn on operations, although the name *Ropey* was only painted on for its return to Canada. Officially handed over to the RCAF on 13 July 1945, KB772 was made available for scrapping on 13 May 1947.

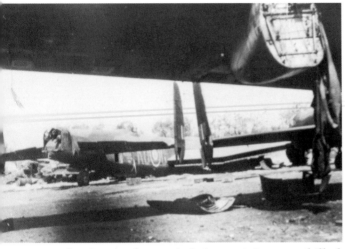

The end of a veteran. While bringing troops home from Italy ME834, KO-G of No. 115 Squadron, burst a tyre on take-off from Bari, causing it to swing into a row of parked aircraft. The 74-sortie veteran completely destroyed HK798, a fellow squadron Lancaster, and PB754 of No. 35 Squadron, which was surgically cut in half. Luckily nobody was seriously injured, but it was said that the incident on 17 August 1945 deprived the British scrap men of three Lancasters.

going home after periods in captivity, were killed when their Lancaster crashed soon after take-off from Juvincourt, France, on 9 May 1945, the first full day after the German surrender.

Some Lancasters were prepared to join the

Tiger Force which had been established to join the war in the Far East, but the Force was never activated as the USAAF's dropping of the atomic bombs on Hiroshima and Nagasaki brought about the Japanese surrender and the end of World War Two.

At the reckoning the cost was high for Bomber Command, with the loss of 55,500 aircrew members and almost 9,000 aircraft. Lancasters flew a total of 156,308 sorties, losing 3,349 in operational and training crashes. The loss rate per sortie (2.2 per cent) was by far the lowest of the RAF's heavy bombers.

After wartime service with Nos 115 and 90 Squadrons, NN761 was transferred to No. 207 Squadron at Spilsby. Here the large post-war style code-letters EM-D were applied in white, as was the underwing serial number, which was appearing for the first time on the heavy bombers.

3. Engineers and Crews

In a letter to Sir Roy Dobson, the managing director of Avro, dated 6 December 1945, Air Chief Marshal Sir Arthur Harris, head of Bomber Command, wrote: 'The Lancaster surpassed all other types of heavy bomber. Not only could it take heavier bomb loads, not only was it easier to handle, not only were there fewer accidents with this than any other type throughout the war, the casualty rate was also considerably below other types. I used the Lancaster alone for those attacks which involved the deepest penetration into Germany and were, consequently, the most dangerous. I would say this to those who placed that shining sword in our hands – without your genius and efforts we could not have prevailed, for I believe that the Lancaster was the greatest single factor in winning the war.'

Those words were a fine tribute to the Lancaster and also to those behind this great aircraft, with Dobson himself the driving force. However, the genius was most certainly Avro's chief designer Roy Chadwick.

The Engineer: Roy Chadwick

The unassuming Roy Chadwick was born in Widnes, Lancashire (now Cheshire) on 30 April 1893 when man's desire to fly was still a dream.

Lancaster designer Roy Chadwick chats to Guy Gibson after their investiture at Buckingham Palace in June 1943. Chadwick was made a CBE while Gibson received the Victoria Cross for his daring leadership on the Dams attack on 16/17 May 1943. There was dismay in aviation circles that, even after the end of the war, Chadwick was never given a knighthood.

By the time of the Wright brothers' first flight in 1903, Chadwick was already building flying models of his own design and even took pencil and paper with him to church every Sunday! His dream came true when he introduced himself to the pioneer aviator Alliott Verdon Roe who was so impressed by the youngster, that he employed him immediately on a salary of one pound per week. Chadwick quickly became assistant to 'A.V.' before eventually being made the Avro chief designer in 1919 at the age of 26. Working with 'A.V.' he had already shared in the design of the Avro 504, which became the standard training aircraft for the Royal Flying Corps during World War One. The design was excellent and the aircraft soldiered on well into the 1930s. It was even used on early radar calibration trials.

By the 1930s Chadwick's designs were being

flown in many parts of the world, with his famous Avian used for private and club flying, while the Tutor became the RAF's principal trainer and its derivatives were operated by many of the world's air forces. In 1934 Chadwick designed a small twin-engined mail-carrying aircraft for Imperial Airways, but it could never have been imagined that this type would be converted to military use and evolve into one of Avro's most famous aircraft, the Anson. From 1935 until 1952 the twin-engined Anson monoplane was in continuous production with almost 11,000 being manufactured.

Soon after the Anson had been designed, the Air Ministry specification for a bomber was met by Chadwick with the design which eventually turned out to be the Avro Manchester. This was plagued by engine problems, but if it had been a success the Lancaster, Chadwick's most famous design, would never have been created. Before the end of the war he had designed the York transport aircraft which, because of its reliability, was used by every one of the British and Commonwealth war leaders. The Lincoln long-range heavy bomber was designed to replace the Lancaster, but World War Two ended before it could be used in anger.

Chadwick was always one step ahead with his thinking and was planning new aircraft early in the development of the jet engine and even speaking about a turboprop engine, which was still a long way in the future. His vision of aircraft flying the Atlantic in a few hours was frowned upon, especially when an eminent Harvard professor had stated that it would be impossible for an aircraft to fly faster that 535 mph!

The war's end saw the return of Lend-Lease aircraft to the United States which left the RAF looking for a long-range maritime reconnaissance type. Chadwick came along with an excellent aircraft which was to become known as the Avro Shackleton. The design was such that the Shackleton remained in RAF service for over 40 years. The atomic age produced a service requirement for an advanced jet bomber capable of delivering its bomb load at targets thousands of miles away. Chadwick's early sketches of a delta-wing design became the basis of the shape which would eventually become the Avro Vulcan. Chadwick would not live to see the Vulcan as, on

23 August 1947, he decided to fly with chief test pilot Bill Thorn in the Avro Tudor II airliner. Tragically, the aircraft crashed during take-off, killing the designer, Thorn and two other crew members. The accident was caused by the aileron controls having been wrongly assembled after overhaul. It was a hard lesson to learn, but today such an error is impossible to duplicate. With that crash the aviation world lost a wealth of irreplaceable experience and Chadwick's death at the age of 54 cut short a career which would have produced even greater designs. He had been awarded the CBE in 1943 for his special modification to the Lancaster design for the famous raid on the German dams and if he had lived he would surely have been knighted. He would have been proud of the honour, but this pride would have been no more than that which he felt for the fine legacy that he had left us in the shape of the Avro Lancaster.

The Crews: Joseph Harold Orrell, Test Pilot

'Jimmy' Orrell was an Avro test pilot during World War Two, working under 'Sam' Brown and his deputy Bill Thorn. Orrell, a pilot of great experience, was born in Liverpool on 9 December 1903, just a few days before the Wright brothers made history. His first test flight in a Lancaster was on 15 April 1942 at Woodford, when he piloted R5517 and later that day flew R5554. Of flight testing the Lancaster he noted, 'The development flights of the Lancaster were fairly brief, partly due to the experience of the Avro Manchester plus the urgency to get the early production aircraft to the RAF.' Nevertheless, due to the excellent design, Chadwick and his team had developed a bomber of quality and performance in record time. Due to the possibility of night air raids, test flying was restricted to daylight hours, which meant long working hours in the summer and as much flying as possible until darkness descended in the winter.

The initial test flight dealt with those things relative to the flight of the aircraft, such as flying controls, engine and propeller operation, undercarriage and flaps, bomb doors, hydraulics, fuel system, electrical services and instrument installation. Presuming that there were no serious snags, the flight would be continued to check performance and handling through the speed range. An initial flight could be completed in 30 to 40 minutes with the help of a flight engineer to record the figures and check the functioning of the services. The main aim was to produce an aircraft with zero time on the ailerons, elevator and rudder, checked over the speed range, thus giving the pilot a maximum trim adjustment in the event of an engine failure or damage to the aircraft by enemy action. After pre-flight checks, the take-off and climb gave a fair indication as to the state of the aircraft. The engineer would go aft to check that the flaps were fully retracted. The next item on the list was to trim the aircraft in level flight cruise conditions, noting the amount of trim required laterally and directionally. Normally rudder and elevator gave little trouble. No lateral trim indicated a good wing and aileron combination, however, this was not always the case as one batch of aircraft needed aileron trims for level flight. In such cases the amount of trim was noted and the engineer would go aft to observe the position of the ailerons in relation to the wing trailing edge. This gave evidence of the amount of wing incidence required to correct the fault. This was achieved by loosening the bolts of the rear section of the wing which were attached to the rear spar. It was then possible to adjust the incidence by inserting slotted washers to the bolts as required. This spate of wing trouble was traced back to the jigs for the main wings. The jig anchorage was found to have moved slightly and regular checks were made after that time. The second and any subsequent flights or tests would repeat the whole test schedule, checking that any previous faults had been cleared. Performance and handling would be covered in all aspects and only then would the aircraft be cleared for

delivery. It is worth recording that the large proportion of production aircraft was cleared for delivery after just two flights. Out of over 4,000 Lancasters test flown at Woodford in possibly 9,000 flights, there was only one fatal accident. It was caused by one of the fuel jettison pipes detaching from the wing while the aircraft was in a maximum speed steep dive. The pipe tore off, hit the tailplane and stripped the elevator skin, causing the aircraft to continue its dive into the ground three miles south of Woodford.

Orrell recalled, 'In my case, I did not have any serious trouble; odd snags did occur which stopped one being too complacent about flying this marvellous aircraft. On one occasion when flying off the west coast, both outboard engines cut out and I returned to Woodford on the inboards. The fault was found to be rain water in the terminal blocks on the engine bulkhead which had shorted the ignition leads during the

Test pilot Jimmy Orrell piloted over 900 Lancasters between 1942 and 1945, including many on their maiden flights. His total number of Lancaster flights was 1,349, after which he went on to make the first flights of ten Avro prototypes including the Canadian C-102 Jetliner. After learning to fly on an Avro 504 Orrell piloted airliners in the pre-war days, but during the war he flew just about every RAF type from Spitfire to Mosquito and American aircraft from the Mitchell to the Liberator, before devoting his time to Avro aircraft.

steep turn. Fortunately the inboard blocks were not too bad, with the cure being made by drain holes in the terminal blocks. The fault was caused by the aircraft standing out on dispersal in a wet period, however, it was better that this happened at Woodford and not in service. On the odd occasion, one or two throttles jammed when closing down power and in this case it was better to leave the throttles in that position and cut the ignition. Engineers would find the cause and rectify the problem before delivery.

'Various changes were made to the Lancaster to suit Bomber Command requirements and these modifications all had to be flight-tested. For instance, the 'Dam Buster' aircraft were not affected by the removal of the bomb doors and the arms fitted for the revolving bomb. However, the change to a Martin mid-upper turret upset the airflow over the tailplane of the Austin-built NN801 at Elmdon. After take-off the pilot found the aircraft difficult to handle and ordered the engineer and an inspector to bale out with fatal consequences for the latter. The pilot then successfully landed back at Elmdon (Birmingham Airport). As the parent firm, Roy Chadwick was concerned and I was sent to Elmdon to investigate the trouble with a few words of caution from the designer. After noting the changes with the new turret, I decided to fly solo knowing that the aircraft was manageable but not pleasant. True enough the aircraft was extremely light in the turn and any real movement caused a fore and aft movement. It was obvious that the elevator was the problem and I could understand the pilot's concern after flying so many Lancasters with excellent controls. Mr Chadwick resolved the problem by the fitting of a strip of material to the top and bottom surfaces of the elevator trailing edge. The cure came after three check flights to determine the amount of strip required. Surprisingly, the fitment of the H_2S blister had no effect on the Lancaster at all and likewise for the large 'Saddle Tank'. Considering the large numbers of Lancasters delivered from Woodford, great credit must go to all of the Avro team as it made the test pilot's job that much easier.

'In conclusion I think that the remarks of Miss Lettice Curtis an Air Transport Auxiliary (ATA) pilot who delivered many aircraft from the factories to the service stations were true, "The Lancaster is too much of a gentleman's aeroplane to test your flying skill as it's straightforward, safe and efficient".' No doubt, a lot of Bomber Command crews would agree.

Jimmy Orrell's log book shows that he flight-tested 900 Lancasters between 15 April 1942 until 23 April 1945 besides fitting in a number of Yorks and a few Lincolns. Jimmy Orrell, OBE, passed away in hospital at Knutsford, Cheshire, on 3 August 1988.

The Lancaster VCs (in order of award)

The Victoria Cross is Britain's highest military decoration. It is awarded for acts of outstanding gallantry to any rank who distinguishes himself in the face of the enemy. Out of the 23 such awards for bomber crews, no fewer than ten of the recipients were Lancaster crew members, although Leonard Cheshire's honour was also associated with other types of aircraft. All awards are listed in the *London Gazette* and include citations with extracts as follows:

John Dering Nettleton

No. 44 (Rhodesia) Squadron, Lancaster R5508 KM-B

The London Gazette, 28 April 1942: 'Squadron Leader Nettleton was the leader of one of two formations of six Lancaster heavy bombers detailed to deliver a low-level attack in daylight on the diesel engine factory at Augsburg in Southern Germany on 17 April 1942. The enterprise was daring, the target of high military importance. To reach it and get back, some 1,000 miles had to be flown over hostile territory.

'Soon after crossing into enemy territory his formation was engaged by 25 to 30 fighters. A running fight ensued. His rear guns went out of action. One by one the aircraft in his formation were shot down until in the end only his and one other remained. The fighters were shaken off but the target was still far distant. There was a formidable resistance to be faced.

'With great spirit and almost defenceless, he held his two remaining aircraft on their perilous course and after a long and arduous flight, mostly at only 50 feet above the ground, he brought them to Augsburg. Here, anti-aircraft fire of great intensity and accuracy was encountered.

The two aircraft came low over the roof tops. Though fired at from point blank range, they stayed the course to drop their bombs true on the target. The second aircraft, hit by flak, burst into flames and crash-landed. The leading aircraft, though riddled with holes, flew safely back to base, the only one of the six to return. Squadron Leader Nettleton, who has successfully undertaken many other hazardous operations, displayed unflinching determination as well as leadership and valour of the highest order.'

John Nettleton (now Wing Commander) was lost, along with his crew, in Lancaster ED331 KM-Z of No. 44 Squadron when it was shot down on the return flight after a raid on Turin on 12/13 July 1943.

Guy Penrose Gibson

No. 617 Squadron, Lancaster ED932 AJ-G
The London Gazette, 28 May 1943: 'Acting Wing Commander Guy Penrose Gibson, DSO, DFC, Reserve of Air Force Officers, No. 617 Squadron.

'This officer served as a night bomber pilot at the beginning of the war and quickly established a reputation as an outstanding operational pilot. In addition to taking the fullest possible share of all normal operations, he made single-handed attacks during his "rest" nights on such highly defended objectives as the German battleship *Tirpitz*, then completing at Wilhelmshaven. When his tour of operational duty was concluded, he asked for a further operational posting and went to a night-fighter unit instead of being posted for instructional duties. In the course of his second operational tour, he destroyed at least three enemy bombers and contributed much to the raising and development of new night-fighter formations.

'After a short period in a training unit he again volunteered for operational duties and returned to night bombers. Both as an operational pilot and as leader of his squadron, he achieved outstandingly successful results and his personal courage knew no bounds. Berlin, Cologne, Danzig, Gydnia, Genoa, Le Creusot, Milan, Nuremberg and Stuttgart were among the targets he attacked by day and by night. On conclusion of his third operational tour, Wing Commander Gibson pressed strongly to be allowed to remain on operations and he was selected to command a squadron then forming

John Nettleton was awarded his Victoria Cross for leading the famous daylight raid on the U-boat engine factory at Augsburg on 17 April 1942.

for special tasks. Under his inspiring leadership, this squadron has now executed one of the most devastating attacks of the war – the breaching of the Möhne and Eder dams.

'The task was fraught with danger and difficulty. Wing Commander Gibson personally made the initial attack on the Möhne Dam. Descending to within a few feet of the water and taking the full brunt of the anti-aircraft defences he delivered his attack with great accuracy. Afterwards he circled very low for 30 minutes drawing the enemy fire on himself in order to leave as free a run as possible to the following aircraft which were attacking the dam in turn.

'Wing Commander Gibson then led the remainder of his force to the Eder Dam, where, with complete disregard for his own safety, he repeated his tactics, and once more drew on himself the enemy fire so that the attack would be successfully developed.

'Wing Commander Gibson has completed 170 sorties, involving more than 600 hours' operational flying. Throughout his operational career, prolonged exceptionally at his own request, he has shown leadership, determination and valour of the highest order.'

Guy Gibson was killed along with his navigator Squadron Leader J.B. Warwick, DFC, when flying Mosquito KB267 AZ-E of No. 627 Squadron. He was acting as 'Master Bomber' for an attack by 227 Lancasters on Rheydt on 19/20 September 1944.

William 'Bill' Reid

No. 61 Squadron, Lancaster LM360 QR-O
The London Gazette 14 December 1943: 'Acting Flight Lieutenant William Reid, RAFVR, No. 61 Squadron.

'On the night of 3 November 1943, Flight Lieutenant Reid was pilot and captain of a Lancaster aircraft detailed to attack Düsseldorf. Shortly after crossing the Dutch coast, the pilot's windscreen was shattered by fire from a Messerschmitt 110. Owing to a failure in the heating circuit, the rear gunner's hands were too cold for him to open fire immediately or to operate his microphone and so give warning of danger, but after a brief delay he managed to return the Messerschmitt's fire and it was driven off.

'During the fight with the Messerschmitt, Flight Lieutenant Reid was wounded in the head, shoulder and hands. The elevator trimming tabs of the aircraft were damaged and it became difficult to control. The rear turret too was badly damaged and the communications system and compasses were put out of action. Flight Lieutenant Reid ascertained that his crew were unscathed, and saying nothing about his own injuries, he continued his mission.

'Soon afterwards, the Lancaster was attacked by

a Focke-Wulf 190. This time, the enemy's fire raked the bomber from stem to stern. The rear gunner replied with his only serviceable gun, but the state of his turret made accurate aiming impossible. The navigator was killed and the wireless operator fatally injured. The mid-upper turret was hit and the oxygen system put out of action. Flight Lieutenant Reid was again wounded and the flight engineer, though hit in the forearm, supplied him with oxygen from a portable supply.

'Flight Lieutenant Reid refused to be turned from his objective and Düsseldorf was reached some 50 minutes later. He had memorised his course to the target and had continued in such a normal manner that the bomb aimer, who was cut off by the failure of the communications system, knew nothing of his captain's injuries or of the casualties to his comrades. Photographs show that, when the bombs were released, the aircraft was right over the centre of the target.

'Steering by the pole star and the moon, Flight Lieutenant Reid then set course for home. He was growing weak from loss of blood. The emergency oxygen supply had given out. With the windscreen shattered, the cold was intense. He lapsed into semi-consciousness. The flight engineer, with some help from the bomb aimer, kept the Lancaster in the air despite heavy anti-aircraft fire over the Dutch coast.

'The North Sea crossing was accomplished. An airfield was sighted. The captain revived, resumed control and made ready to land. Ground mist partially obscured the runway lights. The captain was also much bothered by blood from his head wound getting into his eyes. But he made a safe landing although one leg of the damaged undercarriage collapsed when the load came on.

'Wounded in two attacks, without oxygen, suffering severely from cold, his navigator dead,

Although seriously wounded, Bill Reid brought his badly damaged aircraft and its surviving crew members back to England after the attack on Düsseldorf on 3/4 November 1943. For this amazing feat he was awarded the VC. Upon recovery from his wounds he was invited to visit Avro at Woodford in March 1944 and the photograph shows him, right, with his remaining crew on their way to see new Lancasters rolling off the production line and to spend time talking to the workers.

his wireless operator fatally wounded, his aircraft crippled and defenceless, Flight Lieutenant Reid showed superb courage and leadership in penetrating a further 200 miles into enemy territory to attack one of the most strongly defended targets in Germany, every additional mile increasing the hazards of the long and perilous journey home. His tenacity and devotion to duty were beyond praise.'

Geoffrey Leonard Cheshire

No. 617 Squadron

The London Gazette 8 September 1944: 'Wing Commander Geoffrey Leonard Cheshire, DSO, DFC, Royal Air Force Volunteer Reserve, No. 617 Squadron.

'This officer began his operational career in June 1940. Against strongly-defended targets, he soon displayed the courage and determination of an exceptional leader. He was always ready to accept extra risks to ensure success. Defying the formidable Ruhr defences, he frequently released his bombs from below 20,000 feet. Over Cologne in November 1940, a shell burst inside the aircraft, blowing out one side and starting a fire; undeterred, he went on to bomb the target. About this time, he carried out a number of convoy patrols in addition to his bombing sessions.

'At the end of his first tour of operational duty in January 1941, he immediately volunteered for a second. Again, he pressed home his attacks with the utmost gallantry. Berlin, Bremen, Cologne, Duisburg, Essen and Kiel were among the heavily-defended targets he attacked. When he was posted for instructional duties in January 1942, he undertook four more operational missions.

'He started his third tour in August 1942, when he was given command of a squadron. He led the squadron with outstanding skill on a number of missions before being appointed, in March 1942, as a station commander.

'In October 1943, he undertook a fourth operational tour, relinquishing the rank of Group Captain at his own request so that he could again take part in operations. He immediately set to work as the pioneer of a new method of marking enemy targets involving very low flying. In June 1944, when marking a target in the harbour of Le Havre in broad daylight and without cloud cover, he dived well below the range of the light

The famous Leonard Cheshire meets Norman Jackson, a fellow VC holder who received the award for bravery while flying as flight engineer of a Lancaster detailed to bomb Schweinfurt on 26 April 1944. He attempted to extinguish a fire in the wing after a German night fighter had set the bomber ablaze. Jackson, though wounded, climbed out of the top hatch to attempt to put out the fire, but his parachute partly inflated then caught alight, dragging him off the wing. He landed safely and though badly burned he survived the war.

batteries before releasing his marker bombs, and he came very near to being destroyed by the strong barrage which concentrated on him.

'During his fourth tour which ended in July 1944, Wing Commander Cheshire led his squadron personally on every occasion, always undertaking the most dangerous and difficult task of marking the target alone from a low level in the face of strong defences.

'Wing Commander Cheshire's cold and calculated acceptance of risks is exemplified by his conduct in an attack on Munich in April 1944. This was an experimental attack to test out the new method of target marking at low level against a heavily-defended target situated deep in Reich territory. Munich was selected, at Wing Commander Cheshire's request, because of the formidable nature of its light anti-aircraft and searchlight defences. He was obliged to follow, in bad weather, a direct route which took him over the defences of Augsburg and thereafter he was continuously under fire. As he reached the target, flares were being released by our high-flying aircraft. He was illuminated from above and below. All guns within range opened fire on him.

George Thompson's posthumous award of the VC, was for devotion to duty in the raid against the Dortmund-Ems Canal on 1 January 1945, when he pulled two gunners from their burning turrets. He received severe burns while doing so and died of his injuries three weeks later.

Diving to 700 feet, he dropped his markers with great precision and began to climb away. So blinding were the searchlights that he almost lost control. He then flew over the city at 1,000 feet to assess the accuracy of his work and direct other aircraft. His own was badly damaged by shell fragments but he continued to fly over the target area until he was satisfied that he had done all in his power to ensure success. Eventually, when he set course for base, the task of disengaging himself from the defences proved even more hazardous than the approach. For a full twelve minutes after leaving the target area he was under withering fire, but he came safely through. Wing Commander Cheshire has now completed a total of 100 missions. In four years of fighting against the bitterest opposition he has maintained a record of outstanding personal achievement, placing himself invariably in the forefront of the battle. What he did in the Munich operation was typical of the careful planning, brilliant execution and contempt for danger which has established for Wing Commander Cheshire a reputation second to none in Bomber Command.'

George Thompson (Posthumous Award)

No. 9 Squadron, Lancaster PD377 WS-U
The London Gazette 20 February 1945: '1370700 Flight Sergeant George Thompson, RAFVR No. 9 Squadron, Bomber Command (Deceased)

'This airman was the wireless operator in a Lancaster aircraft which attacked the Dortmund-Ems Canal in daylight on 1 January 1945. The bombs had just been released when a heavy shell hit the aircraft in front of the mid-upper turret. Fire broke out and dense smoke filled the fuselage. The nose of the aircraft was then hit and an inrush of air, clearing the smoke, revealed a scene of utter devastation. Most of the perspex screen of the nose compartment had been shot away, gaping holes had been torn in the canopy above the pilot's head, the inter-communication wiring was severed, and there was a large hole in

the floor of the aircraft. Bedding and other equipment were badly damaged or alight; one engine was on fire.

'Flight Sergeant Thompson saw that the gunner was unconscious in the blazing mid-upper turret. Without hesitation he went down the fuselage into the fire and the exploding ammunition. He pulled the gunner from his turret and, edging his way round the hole in the floor, carried him away from the flames. With his bare hands, he extinguished the gunner's burning clothing. He himself sustained serious burns to his face, hands and legs.

'Flight Sergeant Thompson then noticed that the rear gun turret was also on fire. Despite his own severe injuries he moved painfully to the rear of the fuselage where he found the rear gunner with his clothing alight, overcome by flames and fumes. A second time Flight Sergeant Thompson braved the flames. With great difficulty he extricated the helpless gunner and carried him clear. Again, he used his bare hands, already burnt, to beat out the flames on his comrade's clothing.

'Flight Sergeant Thompson, by now almost fully exhausted, felt that his duty was not yet done. He must report the fate of the crew to the captain. He made the perilous journey back through the burning fuselage, clinging to the side with his burnt hands to get across the hole in the floor. The flow of cold air caused him intense pain and frost-bite developed. So pitiful was his condition that the captain failed to recognise him. Still, his only concern was for the two gunners he had left in the rear of the aircraft. He was given such attention as was possible until a crash-landing was made some forty minutes later.

'When the aircraft was hit, Flight Sergeant Thompson might have devoted his efforts to quelling the fire and so have contributed to his own safety. He preferred to go through the fire to succour his comrades. He knew that he would then be in no position to hear or heed any order which might be given to abandon the aircraft. He hazarded his own life in order to save the lives of others. Young in years and experience, his actions were those of a veteran.

'Three weeks later Flight Sergeant Thompson died of his injuries. One of the gunners unfortunately also died, but the other owes his life to the superb gallantry of Flight Sergeant Thompson, whose single courage and self-sacrifice will ever be an inspiration to the Service.'

Flight Sergeant Thompson's Lancaster was successfully crash-landed at Grolder in Holland. The mid-upper gunner, Sergeant E.J. Potts, died almost immediately, while Flight Sergeant Thompson died on 23 January 1945 in a British Army field hospital.

Robert Anthony Maurice Palmer (Posthumous Award)

No. 109 Squadron (PFF), No. 582 Squadron, Lancaster PB371 60-V

The London Gazette 23 March 1945: 'Acting Squadron Leader Robert Anthony Maurice Palmer, DFC, RAFVR No. 109 Squadron (Classed as 'Missing' at the time of Award)

'This officer completed 110 bombing missions. Most of them involved deep penetration of heavily-defended territory; many were low-level "marking" operations against vital targets; all were executed with tenacity, high courage and great accuracy.

'He first went on operations in January 1941. He took part in the first 1,000-bomber raid on Cologne in 1942. He was one of the first pilots to drop a 4,000-lb bomb on the Reich. It was known that he could be relied upon to press home his attack whatever the opposition and to bomb with great accuracy. He was always selected, therefore, to take part in special operations against vital targets.

'The finest example of his courage and determination was on 23 December 1944 when he led a formation of Lancasters to attack the marshalling yards at Cologne in daylight. He had the task of marking the target, and his formation

Squadron Leader R.A.M. Palmer was another to receive a posthumous VC, after his Lancaster was shot down while he was leading an 'Oboe' attack on Cologne on 23 December 1944. He was carrying out his 110th operation.

had been ordered to bomb as soon had bombs gone from his, the leading aircraft.

'The leader's duties during the final bombing run were exacting and demanded coolness and resolution. To achieve accuracy he would have to fly at an exact height and air speed on a steady course, regardless of opposition.

'Some minutes before the target was reached, his aircraft came under heavy anti-aircraft fire, shells burst all around, two engines were set on fire and there were flames and smoke in the nose and in the bomb bay.

'Enemy fighters now attacked in force. Squadron Leader Palmer disdained the possibility of taking avoiding action. He knew that if he diverged the least bit from his course, he would be unable to utilise the special equipment to the best advantage. He was determined to complete the run and provide an accurate and easily seen aiming-point for the other bombers. He ignored the double risk of fire and explosion in his aircraft and kept on. With his engines developing unequal power, an immense effort was needed to keep the damaged aircraft on a straight course. Nevertheless, he made a perfect approach and his bombs hit the target.

'His aircraft was last seen spiralling to earth in flames. Such was the strength of the opposition that more than half of his formation failed to return.

'Squadron Leader Palmer was an outstanding pilot. He displayed conspicuous bravery. His record of prolonged and heroic endeavour is beyond praise.'

Squadron Leader Palmer died, along with five other members of his crew when the Lancaster was shot down in the target area. The rear gunner, Flight Sergeant R.K. Yeulatt, RAAF, was able to bale out and survived to become a prisoner of war.

Edwin Swales (Posthumous Award)

No. 582 Squadron (PFF), Lancaster PB538 60-M
The London Gazette 24 April 1945: 'Captain Edwin Swales, DFC, SAAF (South African Air Force), No. 582 Squadron (Deceased)

'Captain Swales was "Master Bomber" of a force of aircraft which attacked Pforzheim on the night of 23 February 1945. As "Master Bomber" he had the task of locating the target area with precision and of giving the aiming instructions to the main force of bombers following in his wake.

'Soon after he reached the target area he was engaged by an enemy fighter and one of his engines was put out of action. His rear guns failed. His crippled aircraft was an easy prey to further attacks. Unperturbed, he carried on with his allotted task; clearly and precisely he issued aiming instructions to the main force. Meanwhile the enemy fighter closed the range and fired again. A second engine of Captain Swales' aircraft was put out of action. Almost defenceless, he stayed over the target area issuing his aiming instructions until he was satisfied that the attack had achieved its purpose.

'It is now known that the attack was one of the most concentrated and successful of the war.

'Captain Swales did not, however, regard his mission as completed. His aircraft was damaged. Its speed had been so much reduced that it could only with difficulty be kept in the air. The blind-flying instruments were no longer working. Determined at all costs to prevent his aircraft and crew from falling into enemy hands, he set course for home. After an hour he flew into thin-layered cloud. He kept his course by skilful flying between the layers, but later heavy cloud and turbulent air conditions were met. The aircraft, by now over friendly territory, became more and more difficult to control; it was losing height steadily. Realising that the situation was desperate Captain Swales ordered his crew to bale out. Time was very short and it required all his exertions to keep the aircraft steady while each of his crew moved in turn to the escape hatch and parachuted to safety. Hardly had the last crew member jumped when the aircraft plunged to earth. Captain Swales was found dead at the controls.

'Intrepid in the attack, courageous in the face of danger, he did his duty to the last, giving his life that his comrades might live.'

It was possible that Captain Swales could have survived a crash-landing, but the Lancaster collided with High Tension cables which caused it to dive into the ground. His seven crew members all survived without injury.

Ian Willoughby Bazalgette (Posthumous Award)

No. 635 Squadron (PFF), Lancaster ND811 F2-T
The London Gazette 17 August 1945: 'Acting

Captain Edwin Swales, a South African, serving as 'Master Bomber' on the 23/24 February 1945 attack on Pforzheim, won his VC for continuing to direct the bombing operation even though his Lancaster was burning fiercely. Swales ordered his crew to bale out, but the aircraft went out of control and crashed before he could save himself. The photograph shows Captain Swales, in the light-coloured uniform, and his crew with their aircraft, PB538, 60-M of No. 582 Squadron.

Squadron Leader Ian Willoughby Bazalgette, DFC, RAFVR, No. 635 Squadron (Deceased)

'On 4 August 1944, Squadron Leader Bazalgette was "Master Bomber" of a Pathfinder squadron detailed to mark an important target at Trossy St. Maxim for the main bomber force.

'When nearing the target his Lancaster came under heavy anti-aircraft fire. Both starboard engines were put out of action and serious fires broke out in the fuselage, and the starboard mainplane. The bomb aimer was badly wounded.

'As the deputy "Master Bomber" had already been shot down, the success of the attack depended on Squadron Leader Bazalgette and this he knew. Despite the appaling conditions in his burning aircraft, he pressed on gallantly to the target, marking and bombing it accurately. That the attack was successful was due to his magnificent effort.

'After the bombs had been dropped the Lancaster dived, practically out of control. By expert airmanship and great exertion Squadron Leader Bazalgette regained control. But the port inner engine then failed and the whole of the starboard mainplane became a mass of flames. Squadron Leader Bazalgette fought bravely to bring his aircraft and crew to safety. The mid-upper gunner was overcome by fumes. Squadron Leader Bazalgette then ordered those of his crew who were able to leave by parachute to do so. He remained at the controls and attempted the almost hopeless task of landing the crippled and blazing aircraft in a last effort to save the wounded bomb aimer and helpless gunner. With superb skill, and taking great care to avoid a small French village nearby, he brought the aircraft down safely. Unfortunately, it then exploded and this gallant officer and his two comrades perished. His heroic sacrifice marked the climax of a long career of operations against the enemy. He always chose the more dangerous and exacting roles. His courage and devotion to duty were beyond praise.'

This attack on flying bomb storage sites was highly successful through the accuracy of Squadron Leader Bazalgette's marking at Trossy St Maxim. It was particularly sad that after his excellent crash-landing in a field near the village of Senantes, Squadron Leader Bazalgette, together with Flight Lieutenant I.A. Hibbert, DFC, and Flight Sergeant V.V.R. Leeder, RAAF, were killed as the aircraft blew up before they had a chance to exit it. The remaining crew members successfully evaded capture and eventually reached the Allied lines.

Norman Cyril Jackson

No. 106 Squadron, Lancaster ME669 ZN-O
The London Gazette 26 October 1945: '905192 Sergeant (now Warrant Officer) Norman Cyril Jackson, RAFVR No. 106 Squadron

'This airman was the flight engineer in a Lancaster detailed to attack Schweinfurt on the night of 26 April 1944. Bombs were dropped successfully and the aircraft was climbing out of the target area. Suddenly it was attacked by a fighter at about 20,000 feet. The captain took evading action at once, but the enemy secured many hits. A fire started near a petrol tank on the upper surface of the starboard wing, between the fuselage and the inner engine.

Pathfinder Ian Bazalgette's posthumous Victoria Cross was earned over Trossy-St. Maxim on 4 August 1944. With his Lancaster badly hit, he marked the target accurately and then ordered his crew to abandon the aircraft. With two wounded still aboard he made a good crash landing, but the aircraft exploded, killing Bazalgette and his two remaining crew members.

'Sergeant Jackson was thrown to the floor during the engagement. Wounds which he received from shell splinters in the right leg and shoulder were probably sustained at that time. Recovering himself, he remarked that he could deal with the fire on the wing and obtained his captain's permission to try to put out the flames.

'Pushing a hand fire-extinguisher into the top of his life-saving jacket and clipping on his parachute pack, Sergeant Jackson jettisoned the escape hatch above the pilot's head. He then started to climb out of the cockpit and back along the top of the fuselage to the starboard wing. Before he could leave the fuselage his parachute pack opened and the whole canopy and rigging lines spilled into the cockpit. Undeterred, Sergeant Jackson continued. The pilot, bomb aimer and navigator gathered the parachute together and held on to the rigging lines, paying them out as the airman crawled aft. Eventually he slipped and, falling from the fuselage to the starboard wing, grasped an air intake on the leading edge of the wing. He succeeded in clinging on but lost the extinguisher which was blown away.

'By this time, the fire had spread rapidly and Sergeant Jackson was involved. His face, hands and clothing were severely burnt. Unable to retain his hold he was swept through the flames and over the trailing edge of the wing, dragging his parachute behind. When last seen it was only partly inflated and was burning in a number of places. Realising that the fire could not be controlled, the captain gave the order to abandon the aircraft. Four of the remaining members of the crew landed safely. The captain and rear gunner have not been accounted for.

'Sergeant Jackson was unable to control his descent and landed heavily. He sustained a broken ankle, his right eye was closed through burns and his hands were useless. These injuries, together with the wounds received earlier, reduced him to a pitiable state. At daybreak he crawled to the nearest village, where he was taken prisoner. He bore the intense pain and discomfort of the journey to Dulag Luft with magnificent fortitude. After ten months in hospital he made a good recovery, though his hands require further treatment and are only of limited use.

'This airman's attempt to extinguish the fire and save the aircraft and its crew from falling into enemy hands was an act of outstanding gallantry. To venture outside, when travelling at 200 miles an hour, at a great height and in intense cold, was an almost incredible feat. Had he succeeded in subduing the flames, there was little or no prospect of his gaining the cockpit. The spilling of his parachute and the risk of grave damage to its canopy reduced his chances of survival to a minimum. By his ready willingness to face these dangers he set an example of self-sacrifice which will ever be remembered.'

Canadian Charles Mynarski's posthumous VC was awarded over two years after his death, for his extreme bravery on the night of 12/13 June 1944. His blazing Lancaster was on its way down when the order to abandon was given, but Mynarski saw that the rear gunner was trapped in his jammed turret and went to his aid. The gunner could not be freed and waved to Mynarski to save himself. With his parachute and clothing on fire, Mynarski was cared for by French civilians, but died almost immediately. Amazingly, the trapped rear gunner escaped and survived a heavy parachute landing and it was his report that led to Mynarski's VC. The Canadian Warplane Heritage Lancaster now flies in the colours of Mynarski's aircraft as a tribute to this brave Canadian.

Norman Jackson and four other crew members became prisoners of war. The Lancaster's captain, Flying Officer Mifflin, DFC, and the rear gunner, Flight Sergeant N.H. Jackson, were both killed when the aircraft crashed.

Andrew Charles Mynarski (Posthumous Award)

No. 419 Squadron (RCAF), Lancaster KB726 VR-A
The London Gazette 11 October 1946: 'Pilot Officer Andrew Charles Mynarski (Deceased) Royal Canadian Air Force, No. 419 Squadron RCAF

'Pilot Officer Mynarski was the mid-upper gunner of a Lancaster aircraft detailed to attack a target in Cambrai, France on the night of 12 June 1944. The aircraft was attacked from below and astern by an enemy fighter and ultimately shot down in flames.

'As an immediate result of the attack, both port engines failed. Fire broke out between the mid-upper turret and the rear turret, as well as in the port wing. The flames soon became fierce and the captain ordered the crew to abandon the aircraft.

'Pilot Officer Mynarski left his turret and went towards the escape hatch. He then saw that the rear gunner was still in his turret and apparently unable to leave it. The turret, was in fact, immovable since the hydraulic gear had been put out of action when the port engines failed, and the manual gear had been broken by the gunner in his attempt to escape.

'Without hesitation, Pilot Officer Mynarski made his way through the flames in an endeavour to reach the rear turret and release the gunner. Whilst doing this, his parachute and clothing, up to the waist, were set on fire. All his

efforts to move the turret and free the gunner were in vain. Eventually the rear gunner clearly indicated to him that there was nothing more that he could do and that he should try to save his own life. Pilot Officer Mynarski reluctantly went back through the flames to the escape hatch. There, as in a last gesture to the trapped gunner, he turned towards him, stood to attention in his flaming clothing and saluted, before he jumped from the aircraft. Pilot Officer Mynarski's descent was seen by French people on the ground. Both his parachute and clothing were on fire. He was found by the French, but was so severely burnt that he died of his injuries.

'The rear gunner had a miraculous escape when the aircraft crashed. He subsequently testified that, had Pilot Officer Mynarski not attempted to save his comrade's life, he could have left the aircraft in safety and would, doubtless, have escaped death.

'Pilot Officer Mynarski must have been full aware that in trying to save the rear gunner he was almost certain to lose his own life. Despite this, with outstanding courage and complete disregard for his own safety, he went to the rescue. Willingly accepting the danger, Pilot Officer Mynarski lost his life by a most conspicuous act of heroism which called for valour of the highest order.'

The Lancaster crashed at Gaudiempre near Amiens and, amazingly, the rear gunner, Flying Officer G.P. Brophy, RCAF, was thrown clear and was able to evade capture and eventually return to his unit. In Canada Lancaster FM213 was restored to flying condition by the Canadian Warplane Heritage and painted to represent KB726 VR-A as a tribute to Pilot Officer Mynarski.

CONCLUSION

It has been noted in the past that the compilers of the Victoria Cross citations were not professional writers, with the words being taken from operational reports. The citations should thus be accepted with this in mind.

Without doubt, there were many acts of outstanding bravery amongst Bomber Command crews with the aforementioned being cited in known cases. It will, however, never be known how many other acts of heroism took place before an aircraft crashed killing all on board, or struggled across the enemy coast before going into the sea to be lost for ever. Their stories will never be told, but the courage of all of the brave crews living or dead should not be forgotten.

In 1989 British Aerospace held a dinner to celebrate the 50th Anniversary of the Chadderton factory where the Avro Lancaster was designed and almost 3,000 manufactured. The Author hosted a number of famous personalities associated with the aircraft including L to R 'Penny' Beauchamp; Bill Reid, VC; Bill Townsend; Tony Iveson; the Author; Rod Learoyd, VC; David Penman; Sir Raymond Lygo, (CEO, BAe) and 'Jock' Calder. Reid and Learoyd's V.C.s are well chronicled, but Beauchamp was a Champion of the Lancaster and Commanding Officer of No. 207 Squadron, the third unit to receive the aeroplane. Townsend was one of the Dams pilots. Tony Iveson led one of the flights against the *Tirpitz*. Penman was a flight commander on the daylight raid to Augsburg while Calder carried out tests and made the first attack with the 'Grand Slam' bomb.

4. Accomplishments

The exploits of the Avro Lancaster and its crews during World War Two are legendary, with a service record second to none. In some quarters the Lancaster was seen as just a four-engined version of the Avro Manchester, but nothing could have been further from the truth. Many features of the Manchester's structure were retained, including the complete bomb bay which was unaltered when incorporated into the Lancaster design.

The spreading of four engines across the mainplane, the need for more wing area and the higher aspect ratio to raise the operating altitude, were met by an increase in the dimensions of the outer wings. The basic Manchester centre section was retained as Roy Chadwick could see no reason for change. The use of this component as the Lancaster's centre section was also crucial to meeting the tight schedule set by the Ministry of Aircraft Production for the first flight of the prototype. It later proved to be an inspired decision during the changeover of production from the Manchester to Lancaster.

Besides an increase in operating altitude, there was also a need to improve airfield performance, specifically the take-off distance. With the incorporation of the four Merlins the initial wing span was 100 ft with the positioning of the engines being important as the inboard units had to

The Lancaster's incredible bomb-carrying capacity and variation of load is well illustrated in this photograph of a No. 467 (RAAF) Squadron aircraft's bomb compartment. Aboard are a 4,000-lb 'Cookie', three 1,000-lb bombs, 24 250-lb bombs and six incendiary canisters or Small Bomb Containers (SBCs).

The A&AEE bombing trials aircraft HK543 in a practice drop of a 12,000-lb HC bomb over the Ashley Walk range. When this weapon was cleared for operations it was the largest bomb yet to be carried by an aircraft. The Lancaster had joined the Boscombe Down unit in March 1944, providing valuable information on a wide variety of bombs, including remotely controlled types – note the three aerials under the rear fuselage. The aircraft was sold for scrap on 31 December 1946 after five months in storage.

As with the Manchester, the fuselage was built in five sections, each being fully equipped to assist in ease of maintenance, capable of a complete section change in event of battle damage, and also ease of transportation. The main unit was the centre section with its strong floor forming the roof of the bomb bay. Through the fuselage passed the main spar with girder-type braced ribs to take the inboard engine mounting and undercarriage loads. Forward of the centre section unit was the front fuselage with crew compartment for a pilot, flight engineer, navigator and radio operator. The pilot's canopy and windscreen were also fitted to the forward end of this section with the front of the bomb bay being located below the floor of this unit. Forward of the pilot's cockpit was the fuselage nose unit which incorporated the front gun turret and the bomb aimer's station. Aft of the central unit was the rear centre fuselage housing the aft of the bomb bay and the mid-upper turret. The rear fuselage unit contained the rear gun turret and, immediately forward of this, the centre portion of the tailplane passed through the fuselage section. The mounting for the non-retractable tailwheel was also in this unit. A high proportion of the fuselage length

occupy the Vulture's former placement. The outboard engine position had to be determined by propeller diameter with the engines located as far inboard as possible. Earlier studies of four-engine bomber projects by Avro contributed to the speed in which decisions and selections were made.

The whole Lancaster prototype programme revolved around the new outer wings for which the critical items were the main spars. New sub-frames for the engines had to be adopted for the four Beaufighter engines released by Rolls-Royce for use on the prototype Avro 683. These engines had to fit directly in the outboard positions which had to incorporate a bulkhead kink as on the Beaufighter. For the inboard locations a fireproof bulkhead had to be redesigned to suit the wider nacelle required by the undercarriage retraction.

This sleek 12,000-lb 'Tallboy' was photographed on its transporter in Bardney's bomb storage area on 9 September 1944. This highly successful weapon was used against a variety of targets, from submarine pens to Hitler's Berchtesgaden retreat, with a total of 854 being dropped between June 1944 and April 1945.

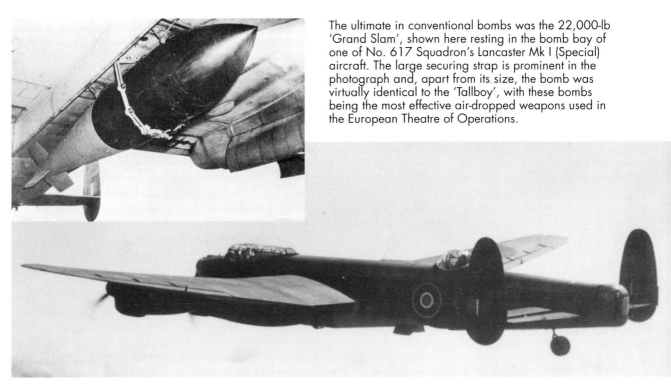

The ultimate in conventional bombs was the 22,000-lb 'Grand Slam', shown here resting in the bomb bay of one of No. 617 Squadron's Lancaster Mk I (Special) aircraft. The large securing strap is prominent in the photograph and, apart from its size, the bomb was virtually identical to the 'Tallboy', with these bombs being the most effective air-dropped weapons used in the European Theatre of Operations.

The 'Grand Slam' trials aircraft, PB995, retained its mid-upper turret while production Mk I (Special) Lancasters had it deleted. The partly exposed weapon extends beyond the bomb compartment with two if its fins being visible. The first live practice drop of the bomb produced a crater 124 ft in diameter and 30 ft deep. The following day, 14 March 1945, the same pilot, Squadron Leader C.C. 'Jock' Calder, delivered one on the Bielefeld viaduct with an excellent result. Before the end of the war 41 'Grand Slams' had been used.

was of a constant cross-section, with the heavier frames being located at the transport joints thus enabling similar tooling to be used for many of the frames and stringers.

A few deficiencies

Undoubtedly, the Lancaster was the finest bomber to serve during World War Two with its crews being more than proud to fly it. However, if any criticism could be levelled at the Lancaster it was the crew's survivability rate. The cavernous bomb bay meant that the wing main spar crossed the fuselage above the floor, making entry to and exit from the forward crew stations a difficult operation even in normal circumstances, but to have to abandon the aircraft in an emergency proved very demanding. The forward parachute exit was located in the extreme nose while the rear door on the starboard side of the aircraft was not recommended for a bale out due to the closeness

of the tailplane. In the event of a wheels-up or water landing there were three emergency exits in the top of the aircraft, but these were not for use as parachute escapes. The losses of Lancasters in action were fewer than the other heavies used by Bomber Command, but in terms of crew members lost the comparison was balanced.

The bomb compartment at 33-ft 3-in long, was almost half the length of the Lancaster and at 5-ft 6-in wide the scope for carrying a large variety of bombs was considerable. In most cases the aircraft operated in its role without any changes to the structure and out of the total number of 7,377 Lancasters produced, fewer than 60 had to be modified to carry special weapons. The first of these conversions was for the 'Capital Ship' bomb, which was an unusually shaped weapon of 5,600 lb which required the aircraft to have an overload take-off weight of 67,000 lb. The 'Upkeep' weapon used on the Dams raid was

As peacetime returned, Lancasters continued to be in the news and none more so than *Aries*, PD328 of the Empire Air Navigation School (EANS) at Shawbury, which made a number of long distance flights particularly to solve the problems of over-sea navigation. These operations had commenced in standard Lancaster configuration in October 1944, but the aircraft was later modified with a streamlined nose and tail fairings in place of the turrets. It continued to provide valuable data until it was eventually retired and sold for scrap on 11 August 1948.

cylindrical, almost 50 in in diameter and weighed 9,250 lb. The aircraft involved had their bomb doors removed, with special arms mounted in the bay to carry the bomb, or mine as it was classed. An hydraulic motor had to be fitted complete with drive gear in order to rotate the weapon giving it the necessary back-spin, and fairings fore and aft of the bomb bay were fitted to reduce drag. The mid-upper gun turret was also removed to reduce weight and trials

showed that despite the drastic modifications to the aircraft, the handling of the machine was unaffected. The rest is history.

The designer of the 'Upkeep' weapon, Dr Barnes Wallis, worked closely with Roy Chadwick on this project and this association was to last until the latter's death. On two further occasions their liaison produced the 'Tallboy' and 'Grand Slam' deep penetration bombs which were carried by Lancasters. Their penetration into the ground was designed to create a mini earthquake with the aerodynamic shape giving the highest possible speed from release to impact.

Carrying out similar navigation operations over the vast expanses of Canada was FM211 *Zenith* of the RCAF's Central Navigation School (CNS). The machine was one of five converted to navigation trainers after the war by Fairey Aviation Limited. These aircraft were fitted with de-icer boots on the wings and tail, with two 400-Imp gal fuel tanks in the bomb compartment plus the latest in navigational equipment. Although FM211 did not see war service, it did serve for ten years before being declared surplus on 8 May 1956.

This aircraft is the Austin Motors-built Lancaster Mk VII RT684 *Polaris*, of the Empire Air Navigation School – later Central Navigation School. When completed at Longbridge, the aircraft wore the white with black undersides colour scheme designed for Far East aircraft. After a major overhaul, it appeared in the grey and black scheme shown here and wearing the code letters FGG-Q. It was finally Struck off Charge on 28 February 1951.

The tail fins on these bombs were set at angles to introduce a spin during the fall. The Lancaster was already able to carry both 8,000-lb and 12,000-lb high capacity (HC) bombs with slight modification so no changes were needed to accommodate the 12,000-lb 'Tallboy'. This modification consisted of strengthening the main bomb beams and bulging the bomb doors. The massive 22,000-lb 'Grand Slam' far exceeded the normal Lancaster bomb load and the weapon's dimensions meant that even within modified bomb doors it could not be enclosed. In order to minimise centreline weight, the nose and mid-upper turrets had to be removed. A fuel management system had to be introduced to keep fuel in the outer wing tanks as long as possible in order to reduce possible wing bending. The only problem would arise if an aircraft had to return to base with the bomb still on board as the Air Ministry decreed that, due to

Above: The Photographic Reconnaissance version of the Lancaster did valuable work surveying Central and West Africa between 1946 and 1952, but the greatest area of operations was in the east with Kenya, Uganda and Tanganyika (now Tanzania) extensively covered. No. 82 Squadron flew these aircraft and in the photograph TW901, a PR.Mk I, is shown parked at Nairobi in 1952.

Until the arrival of Avro Shackletons, Lancasters proved to be an excellent stopgap for Coastal Command's maritime reconnaissance duties. Operating in Palestine and, later, Malta, No. 38 Squadron flew patrols in the eastern Mediterranean, with its aircraft including this GR.Mk III, SW336.

NG465, a Rolls-Royce test-bed, was fitted with a Dart turboprop engine in the nose in October 1947. It later flew with a large rig around the engine to induce icing conditions from a water spray. The trials must have been successful as the Dart became one of the world's most popular and reliable turboprop engines. The aircraft had seen wartime service with a number of squadrons before being allocated to Rolls-Royce. In the background on the airfield at Hucknall are a Fairey Barracuda and the Merlin-600 trials Lancaster, PP791.

its high cost, the weapon must not be jettisoned. A strengthened undercarriage and a clearance for a high landing weight was obtained if a 'Grand Slam' had to be returned. Altogether 41 'Grand Slams' were dropped in anger while no fewer than 854 'Tallboys' were used on operations.

The RAF's four-engined bombers, the Stirling, Halifax and Lancaster, all served with distinction, but it was the latter which proved to be the outstanding machine in every respect. The Handley Page Halifax was capable of carrying a maximum bomb load of 13,000 lb for 1,260 miles

A fine flying shot of the Lancaster Mk II LL735, which was one of a number of the type used by engine manufacturers for tests on a variety of new powerplants. This machine had the Metrovick F.2/4 Beryl axial-flow turbojet in its tail and in earlier trails the prototype Lancaster BT308 had flown with a Metrovick F.2/1 installed in a similar position.

This Lancaster ASR.Mk III, SW377, carries an airborne lifeboat while operating as CJ-B of No. 203 Squadron of Coastal Command. The aircraft was later reclassified as a GR.Mk III, but retained the capability of carrying the lifeboat.

or a range of 2,400 miles with a much reduced load. The Short Stirling's maximum bomb load was a respectable 14,000 lb, but only with a range of 590 miles and for a trip of 2,000 miles the load reduced to 3,500 lb. By comparison the Lancaster's average bomb load was 14,000 lb which could be hauled 1,660 miles, reducing to 10,000 lb for a range of 2,250 miles. Even with a 22,000-lb 'Grand Slam' the aircraft had an operational range of 1,040 miles. In the reckoning, the productivity of the Lancaster was far greater than the other machines with regard to bomb tonnage dropped against aircraft lost, with the Stirling at 41 tons, the Halifax 51 tons and the Lancaster a massive 132 tons.

Its excellent power-to-weight ratio gave the Lancaster outstanding performance and the manoeuvrability for such a large aircraft was second to none. The robust structure allowed its pilots to carry out stressful 'corkscrewing' to evade fighters or searchlights and it is known that Lancasters were barrel-rolled or looped several times; a tribute to the pilots' faith in them.

Chadwick's carefully thought-out design and construction methods made a very produceable aircraft with equipped sections yielding benefits in maintenance, repair and replacement.

After the war in Europe had ended there was a speedy run-down of Bomber Command with some of the squadrons being disbanded as quickly as they were formed during the expansion. Canadian-built Lancasters soon returned home and then went on to provide excellent service in the RCAF for a further 20 years before eventually being withdrawn from front-line duties.

The last Lancaster to be built, TW910 a

In the continuous search for improved armament, Lancaster LL780/G completed a number of trials at the Royal Aircraft Establishment at Farnborough with pairs of 20-mm cannon installed in remotely controlled barbettes in upper and lower positions. The redesigned rear fuselage contained a fire controller's station, while the small radome at the rear contained the Automatic Gun-Laying (AGL(T)) equipment. The Lancaster in the background was JB456, which had been used for trials with twin 20-mm cannon in a Bristol turret. The former was also seen in the code DF-N with the Central Bomber Establishment.

Flight Refuelling Limited of Tarrant Rushton pioneered air-to-air refuelling techniques, with the RAF supporting the requirement for tanker aircraft to refuel long-range bombers. The Lancaster with the civil registration G-AHJW, ex-ED866 had served with Nos 97 and 619 Squadrons and No. 5 LFS before being allocated to FRL as a trials aircraft. The refuelling hose can be seen trailing from a ventral hatch while it awaits the receiver aircraft. The FRL tanker Lancasters did sterling work during the Berlin Airlift carrying much needed fuel to the beleaguered city. Sadly, G-AHJW was destroyed in a crash near Andover on 22 November 1948.

Mk I (FE), was delivered by Armstrong Whitworth to the RAF on 2 February 1946 and served with Nos 207 and 115 Squadrons before being Struck off Charge on 6 March 1950. It seemed strange to accept an aircraft which was surplus to requirements, but with production of Lancasters planned well into 1946, the war ended sooner than expected with the dropping of the atomic bombs and although many Lancasters were cancelled, the immediate cessation of production would have thrown the aircraft industry into turmoil.

The first Lancaster to go onto the British Civil Register actually did so while the war was at its height as it was on 11 November 1943 when the Mk I which would have been DV379 for the RAF was registered to BOAC as G-AGJI. This aircraft was evaluated for airline use with route-proving work leading to the development of the Lancastrian. It was decided to convert a number of Lancaster production batches into Lancastrians as nine to twelve-seat airliners. The prototype flew for the first time on 17 January 1945 in the hands of Avro test pilot Jimmy Orrell. This aircraft, G-AGLF was delivered from Woodford to BOAC at Croydon on 18 February 1945 and the airline continued to use Lancastrians on its long-range routes until September 1950. Others of the type saw service with the RAF and foreign airlines and later provided valuable service as test-beds.

Developments in service equipment for the RAF saw Lancasters in a variety of specialised roles including *Aries* of the Empire Air Navigation School which established a number of records during a series of long-distance flights. The Central Signals Establishment had the Lancaster *Iris* which was equipped with every conceivable radio and radar aid, while extensive developments in blind-bombing and gunnery were conducted by *Thor* of the Empire Air Armament School.

A small number of Lancaster Mk Is was converted into photographic reconnaissance aircraft with the designation PR.Mk I. These aircraft were operated by No. 541 Squadron, which was reformed into No. 82 Squadron on 1 October 1946, and No. 683 Squadron. Both of these units completed extensive aerial survey work in East, West and Central Africa, Egypt and Arabia. These squadrons flew Lancasters until the end of 1953, when No. 683 was disbanded, while No. 82 went into the jet age by receiving Canberras. Other squadrons, including Nos 37, 40, 70 and 104 operated Lancasters from Egypt and Palestine on a variety of duties which covered the whole of that area, the Suez Canal and the sea approaches.

American aircraft which had been in RAF service under the wartime Lend-Lease agreement had to be returned to the United States after the war, which left Coastal Command in dire need of long-range maritime patrol aircraft. The Lancaster proved to be the solution and suitably modified aircraft became the main equipment of Coastal Command. Some Lancasters were developed for the maritime reconnaissance (MR) role while others became General Reconnaissance (GR) types. It was after the war that the prefix of the type, 'B' for bomber, which had originated in wartime, started to be used by Avro among others, so that a Lancaster Mk III became the B.Mk 3 or B.3 as it was abbreviated to. With the modifications the Coastal aircraft became MR.Mk 3s (MR.3s) and GR.Mk 3s (GR.3s) and a further version for the ASR role equipped with a Cunliffe-Owen lifeboat was known as the ASR.Mk 3 (ASR.3).

The last Lancasters to serve overseas were the MR.3s of No. 38 Squadron which operated from Luqa, Malta. No. 38's last Lancaster, RF273, returned to the UK in February 1954 after the Squadron had started to receive Avro Shackletons. On 10 October 1956 an RAF Press Release stated that just five days later, the Lancaster would be officially withdrawn from its service. A farewell ceremony duly took place at St Mawgan in Cornwall on Monday 15 October 1956 when RF325, from the School of Maritime Reconnaissance, was retired and flown away to Wroughton, Wiltshire, to be scrapped.

Apart from the Canadian Lancasters, others were used by the air forces of Argentina and Egypt, while the French Navy operated the aircraft in the Mediterranean area, North Africa and the South Pacific. The Russians used two Lancasters which were made flyable by using spares from the six aircraft which had force-landed in the country during the September 1944 attack on the *Tirpitz*. Another operator was the Royal Swedish Air Force which flew the aircraft as an engine test-bed.

British aero engine developments kept a number of Lancasters active as every major manufacturer used the type as a test-bed for piston, turboprop and jet engine trials. The Lancaster was also widely used as both a tanker and receiver in air-to-air fuel transfer experiments carried out by Flight Refuelling Limited and in 1948 two of the company's tanker aircraft did sterling service during the Berlin Airlift. Lancasters were used in many trials from glider towing to target tug and all with the usual efficiency.

The excellent design of the Lancaster enabled the 39,000 lb maximum take-off weight of the prototype to be cleared to 60,000 lb by the time the second prototype was available for testing. By November 1942 production Lancasters were operating at weights up to 63,000 lb, then in May 1944 both the Marks I and III were approved to fly at 65,000 lb. Incredibly, by January 1945 the aircraft was operated with overload weights of 72,000 lb and all of these weight improvements were achieved with little technical change to the original design.

Despite the variety of roles performed, it is as a bomber that the Lancaster is synonymous, and it is a fine tribute to the aircraft and its brave crews that two examples have been kept flying. The Battle of Britain Memorial Flight in the UK proudly displays its Lancaster at air shows and various ceremonial occasions, while across the Atlantic the Canadian Warplane Heritage Museum also flies a beautifully rebuilt aircraft. Both of these aircraft serve to perpetuate the memory of those young men and their magnificent flying machine.

Lancaster war record

In a letter dated 20 October 1945 from Group Captain S.P.A. Patmore, OBE, of Bomber Command Headquarters, High Wycombe to the Headquarters of A.V. Roe & Company Limited at Chadderton, the following statistics were recorded:

(a) Total tonnage of High Explosive bombs dropped by Lancaster aircraft on primary targets was 608,612. This figure is enough to fill a goods train 345 miles long! However, the total tonnage figure is for bombs actually dropped as the figure for bombs uplifted or despatched in Lancasters is not included. With an average of four tons per aircraft this translates to over 150,000 sorties which would consume 228 million Imperial gallons of fuel.

(b) The total number of incendiaries dropped by Lancasters was 51,513,106

(c) Total tons of food and supplies dropped to the Dutch by Lancaster was 6,672

(d) Total number of ex-prisoners of war repatriated by Lancasters was 74,178

Note: The High Explosive figure quoted above is almost exactly two-thirds of the total tonnage dropped by the whole of Bomber Command from March 1942 to May 1945.

This table lists all of the Lancasters which completed 100 or more operational missions.

Type	Serial	Sqn	Codes	Ops
Mk I	R5868	83/467	OL-Q/	
			PO-S	137
Mk I	W4964	9	WS-J	106
Mk III	DV245	101	SR-S	119
Mk I	DV302	101	SR-H	121
Mk I	ED588	97/50	None/	
			VN-G	128
Mk III	ED611	44/463	KM-J/	
			JO-T	113
Mk III	ED860	156/61	None/	
			QR-N	130

Type	Serial	Sqn	Codes	Ops
Mk III	ED888	103/576 /103	PM-M/ UL-V[2]/ UL-M[2]/ PM-M[2]	140
Mk III	ED905	103/166 /550	PM-X/ AS-X/ BQ-F	100+
Mk III	EE136	9/189	WS-R/ CA-R	109
Mk III	EE139	100/550	HW-R/ BQ-B	121
Mk III	EE176	7/97/61	None/ OF-N/ OF-O/ QR-M	122
Mk III	JB138	61	QR-J	123
Mk III	JB603	100	HW-E	111
Mk III	JB663	106	ZN-A	111
Mk I	LL772	626/101	UM-F[2]/ SR-R/ SR-R[2]	121
Mk I	LL806	15	LS-J	134
Mk I	LL843	467/61	PO-T/ QR-A	118
Mk I	LL885	622	GI-J	113
Mk I	LM227	576	UL-I[2]	100
Mk III	LM550	166/153	AS-B/ P4-C	107
Mk III	LM594	576	UL-G[2]/ UL-A[2]	104
Mk I	ME746	166	AS-R[2]/ AS-C	116
Mk I	ME758	12	PH-N	108
Mk I	ME803	115	A4-D/ KO-L/IL-B	105
Mk I	ME801	576	UL-C[2]/ UL-N[2]/ UL-W[2]	114+
Mk I	ME812	166/153	AS-F/P4-F	105
Mk III	ND458	100	HW-A/ HW-A[2]	127
Mk III	ND578	44	KM-Y	121
Mk III	ND644	100	HW-N	115
Mk III	ND709	35/635/ 405	TL-M/ F2-J/ LQ-G	111
Mk III	ND875	7/156	None/ GT-N	100+
Mk III	NE181	75	AA-M/ JN-M	101
Mk III	PA990	626	UM-R[2]	105
Mk III	PA995	550	BQ-V/ BQ-K	101
Mk III	PB150	625	CF-V/ CF-V[2]	100+

5. Variants

Lancaster Variants

The Prototypes: The first prototype, BT308, had a wing span of 100 ft and was powered by four Rolls-Royce Merlin X engines. It initially had a large central fin, but this was later deleted, larger fins being fitted and the tailplane span being increased to 33 ft. A dorsal turret was not fitted. Its first flight was on 9 January 1941.

The second prototype, DG595, had a new tail configuration and a dorsal turret with power being supplied by four Merlin XXs. This fully productionised aircraft made its maiden flight on 13 May 1941.

Lancaster Mk I: Wing span 102 ft and powered by four Merlin XX, 22 or 24 engines. First production aircraft maiden flight 31 October 1941.

Lancaster Mk I or B.Mk I (Special): Using Modification Number 1693, this Mark was cleared to carry bomb loads in excess of 12,000 lb. The maximum take-off weight could be up to 72,000 lb.

Lancaster Mk I or B.Mk I (FE): Tropicalised version for use by the 'Tiger Force' against Japan.

Lancaster PR.Mk I: Photographic reconnaissance version.

Lancaster Mk I (Western Union): Under the Western Union agreement, 54 Lancasters were supplied to the French navy (Aéronavale). Of these, 32 were Mk Is while 22 were Mk VIIs.

However, with the removal of their mid-upper turrets and modifications to suit the French requirements, these aircraft all became known as the Mk I (Modified).

Lancaster Mk II prototype: Bristol Hercules VI radial engines replaced the Merlins on the Mk II with the serial numbers DT810 and DT812 being allocated for two prototypes. The flight tests of the first aircraft were so successful that there was no requirement for the second aircraft. The first flight of DT810 was made on 26 November 1941.

Lancaster Mk II: The radial-engined Lancaster was ordered into production after the success of the prototype, with Armstrong Whitworth Aircraft (AWA) manufacturing 300 of this type. As on the prototype, the production aircraft were powered by the Bristol Hercules VI, with the Hercules XVI being introduced at a later stage. The Rotol propellers on the Hercules engines rotated to the left as opposed to all Merlin-powered Lancasters which had airscrews rotating in a clockwise direction. Production aircraft first flight 2 September 1942.

Lancaster Mk III prototype: The Mark III was identical to the Mark I, with the exception of its American Packard licence-built version of the Rolls-Royce Merlin. The first Lancaster to be fitted with the American Merlin 28 was R5849, although the recognised prototype for the Mark III was W4114 which carried out most of the development flying and also included trials of the US-Stromberg carburettor.

Lancaster Mk III: Packard Merlins 28, 38 or 224 provided the power for this type. All other details are as the Mark I.

Lancaster Mk III Type 464 Provisioning: The Type Number for the 23 aircraft converted to carry the 'Upkeep' mine for the famous attack on the Ruhr Dams in May 1943.

Lancaster ASR.Mk III: Conversion of Lancasters for the Air-Sea Rescue role was undertaken by Cunliffe-Owen of Eastleigh, Southampton. These aircraft, powered by Merlin 224s, were modified to carry the Cunliffe-Owen Airborne Lifeboat Mk IIA.

Lancaster GR.Mk III/MR.Mk III: Lancasters were converted to the maritime reconnaissance role to fill the gap after Coastal Command Consolidated Liberators were returned to the

In post-war service Canadian-built Lancaster Mk Xs were much modified as KB839 shows. The aircraft became a Mk 10AR (Arctic Reconnaissance) aircraft of the RCAF's No. 408 Squadron based at Rockliffe, Ontario. It had flown a number of bombing operations in 1945 while serving as VR-D with No. 419 (RCAF) Squadron (a photograph of KB839's mid-upper turret appears in Appendix 2). The aircraft ceased flying in 1964 and is on display at the Canadian Armed Forces Base at Greenwood, but the engines have been sent to the Canadian Warplane Heritage Museum to help keep its Lancaster flying.

USA when the Lend-Lease programme ended. The type continued in this task until 1956.

Lancaster Mk IV: This Mark number was originally allocated to the Type 694 which later became known as the Avro Lincoln. This large bomber made its first flight on 9 June 1944, but its entry into service was delayed by the full-scale production programme of the Lancaster, with the war ending before the Lincoln could be used in anger.

Lancaster Mk V: Still using the Avro Type 694 designation, this aircraft became the Lincoln Mk II

Lancaster Mk VI: It was proposed to increase the performance of the Mk III by installing the higher-powered Merlin 85 or 87 engines with two aircraft, DV170 and DV199, being allocated to Rolls-Royce for engine fitment and flight testing. Seven others were modified to this standard for service trials, but one of these, ND479, crashed during stick-force tests before it could be allocated to a squadron. Of those remaining, JB713 flown by Nos 7, 405 and 635 Squadrons was lost on operations on the night of 18/19 August 1944 while serving with the last of these units. JB675 also served with the same squadrons before returning to Rolls-Royce at Hucknall where it provided excellent service as a test-bed for a variety of engines. Nos 83, 7 and 635 Squadrons operated ND418 before it went on

As a result of the Western Union treaty in March 1948 the French identified a requirement to equip the Aéronavale with the Lancaster for maritime patrol duties. Low-houred aircraft were taken from storage, with the 54 required being taken from No. 38 MU at Llandow in South Wales. After being converted by Avro, the first machine was delivered in December 1951. The aircraft pictured here, WU-40, ex-PA432, served extensively in North Africa until it was retired in June 1961.

to No. 582 Squadron, then the Royal Aircraft Establishment (RAE) at Farnborough, ending its career with the Bomb Ballistics Unit (BBU). Armstrong Whitworth Aircraft and Power Jets Limited used ND784 for engine tests before it was eventually scrapped in 1951. No. 635 Squadron, the most experienced operator of the Mk VI, also flew ND558 which was then passed on to the BBU while ND673 was the most successful, completing 23 operations before being allocated to the RAE where it was flown until January 1947 then put up for disposal.

Lancaster Mk VII (Interim): Although this designation was not officially recognised, it became generally accepted for 50 Lancaster Mk Is built by Austin which were to be fitted with the Martin gun turret in the mid-upper position, although sited slightly forward of the normal location. The late delivery of these new turrets from the USA meant that standard Frazer-Nash turrets had to be installed in the position directly over the rear of the bomb bay. The aircraft, with serial numbers NX548 to NX589 and NX603 to NX610 entered RAF service as Mark Is.

Lancaster Mk VII/Mk VII (FE): Also known as the B.Mk VII and B.Mk VII (FE) these aircraft were built exclusively by Austin and were identified by the Martin mid-upper turrets with twin 0·5 inch machine-guns. Located further forward than the Frazer-Nash turret on the Marks I and III, the Martin was electrically rather than hydraulically operated. The FE designation applied to those aircraft tropicalised for use by the 'Tiger Force'.

Lancaster Mk VII (Western Union): Twenty-two of the 54 Lancasters supplied to the French Aéronavale were Mark VIIs, but with the removal of the mid-upper gun turret they were designated Lancaster Mk I (Modified). A further five of the type were ordered by the French Government to be used by a civilian rescue agency.

Lancaster Mk VIII: This Mark number was reserved for developments of the Lancaster made by the parent company, A.V. Roe & Company Limited.

Lancaster Mk IX: Reserved for Lancasters developed in Britain.

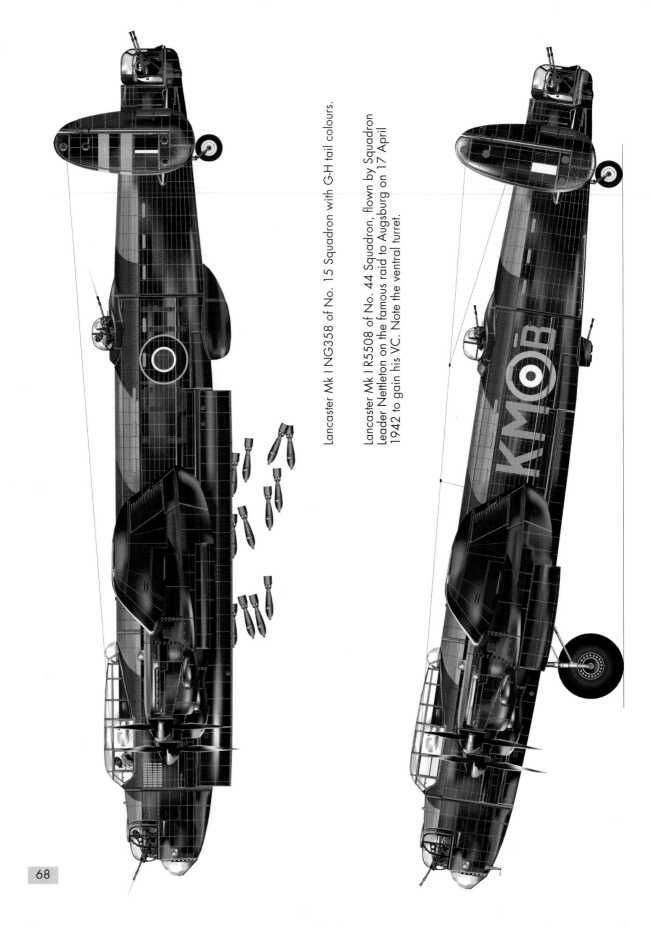

Lancaster Mk I NG358 of No. 15 Squadron with G-H tail colours.

Lancaster Mk I R5508 of No. 44 Squadron, flown by Squadron Leader Nettleton on the famous raid to Augsburg on 17 April 1942 to gain his VC. Note the ventral turret.

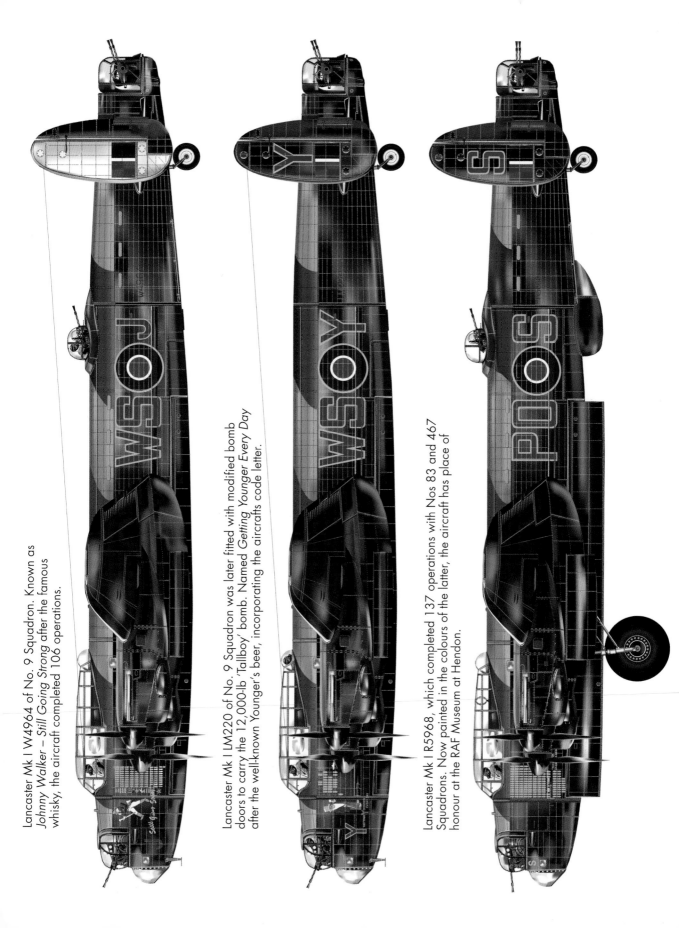

Lancaster Mk I W4964 of No. 9 Squadron. Known as *Johnny Walker – Still Going Strong* after the famous whisky, the aircraft completed 106 operations.

Lancaster Mk I LM220 of No. 9 Squadron was later fitted with modified bomb doors to carry the 12,000-lb 'Tallboy' bomb. Named *Getting Younger Every Day* after the well-known Younger's beer, incorporating the aircrafts code letter.

Lancaster Mk I R5968, which completed 137 operations with Nos 83 and 467 Squadrons. Now painted in the colours of the latter, the aircraft has place of honour at the RAF Museum at Hendon.

The ex-RAF Lancasters ordered by Argentina were taken out of storage and, after overhaul and repaint, were delivered to the Fuerza Aérea Argentina between May 1948 and January 1949. The 15 aircraft were little used, apart from emphasising the power of the military regime. B-034, ex-PA350, was destroyed in a crash in 1963.

Lancaster Mk X: This designation was allocated to Canadian-built Lancasters manufactured by Victory Aircraft at Malton, Ontario. A total of 430 of the Packard-Merlin powered Mark X were produced with all airframe sections being interchangeable with those of their British-built counterparts.

Lancaster Projects: A number of design projects for the Lancaster were studied by Roy Chadwick and his team including a High-Altitude version with Rolls-Royce Merlin 60 engines in a design dated 29 July 1941. A High-Speed aircraft was planned, but did not go beyond the basic design stage. A more serious project was given the Type Number 684, known as the Stratosphere Bomber, to be powered by Merlin XXs, but with a slave Merlin 45 engine mounted internally in the fuselage which would be supercharged and fitted with a blower to increase the air pressure on the carburettors of the main engines. A pressure cabin would be provided for the crew allowing operations over 40,000 ft. It was estimated that with a cruising speed of 330 mph at 40,000 ft the aircraft could carry a 4,000-lb bomb load for a range of some 2,300 miles. Varying bomb loads of up to 12,000 lb could be carried over shorter distances with the maximum weight of the aircraft being 60,000 lb. It was planned that after delivering its bomb

load the machine would climb to its absolute ceiling of 50,300 ft for its return to base. The Avro 684 would have been unarmed and would have relied on its altitude to escape any attackers. The initial project drawing was dated 16 August 1941 and feasibility studies were undertaken, but some months later, the improving war situation and the success of the production Lancasters meant that this interesting project would never go further than the studies.

Overseas operators

Canada: Victory Aircraft built 430 Lancaster Mk Xs from 1943 to 1945 at the rate of four aircraft per week. The first of the type to arrive in Britain was KB700 which flew in on 6 August 1943. The Lancaster Mk Xs were supplied to No. 6 (RCAF) Group serving in England, with 105 being lost by the four squadrons which operated the aircraft. A total of 288 Lancaster Mk Xs returned to Canada at the end of the war, with the balance of the production awaiting delivery, although six of the type had been transferred to Trans Canada Airlines for the long-range transport role. In the post-war years the Lancasters would be extensively modified to undertake a wide variety of roles required by the RCAF. The Roman-style Mark numbering system used by the wartime RAF was changed to Arabic numbers during the 1949–50 period.

Pictured shortly before it was lost in an accident on 8 May 1956, the Swedish Lancaster, 80001, ex-RA805, provided that country with excellent data on the Stal Dovern turbojet engine project. However, the engine did not perform as expected and the aircraft subsequently flew with a de Havilland Ghost until it was written-off.

The famous 'G for George', Lancaster W4783, was presented to Australia and arrived at Amberley airfield after its long flight from England on 8 November 1944. It was soon given the RAAF serial number A66-2, before going on to raise a large amount of money for the war effort by flying fare-paying members of the public! The aircraft is now on display in the Australian War Memorial Hall at Canberra, looking resplendent in its wartime colours.

Approximately 100 aircraft were put into service with their respective designations for the roles involved.

Lancaster Mk 10AR: Arctic Reconnaissance version with a lengthened nose and additional radar and camera equipment.

Lancaster Mk 10BR: For bomber reconnaissance duties.

Lancaster Mk 10DC: Two aircraft were converted for drone-carrying trials.

Lancaster Mk 10MR/MP: Initially known as MR for maritime reconnaissance work, the

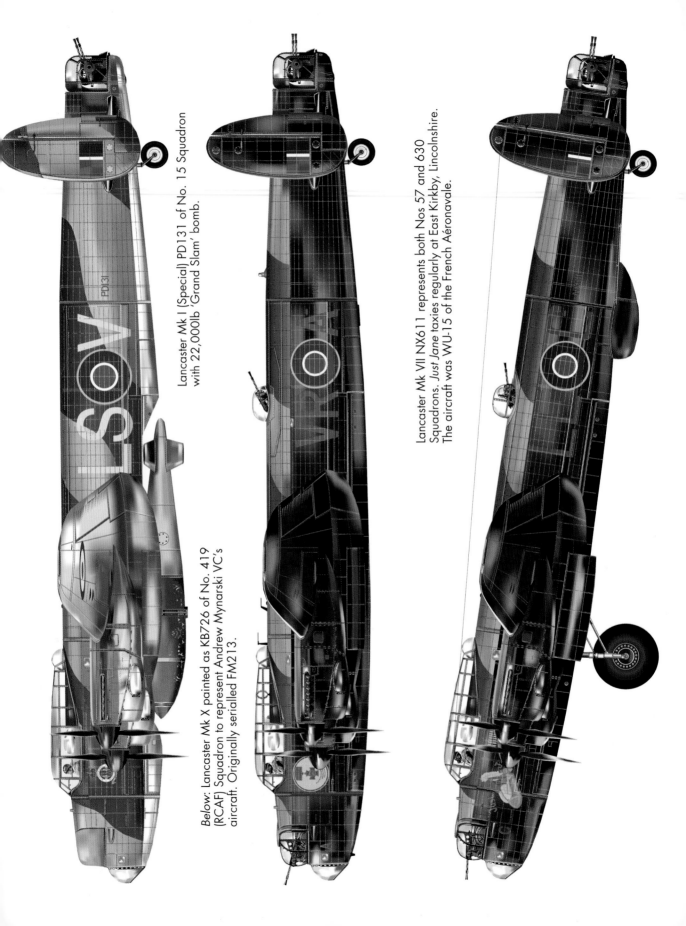

Lancaster Mk I (Special) PD131 of No. 15 Squadron with 22,000lb 'Grand Slam' bomb.

Below: Lancaster Mk X painted as KB726 of No. 419 (RCAF) Squadron to represent Andrew Mynarski VC's aircraft. Originally serialled FM213.

Lancaster Mk VII NX611 represents both Nos 57 and 630 Squadrons. *Just Jane* taxies regularly at East Kirkby, Lincolnshire. The aircraft was WU-15 of the French Aéronavale.

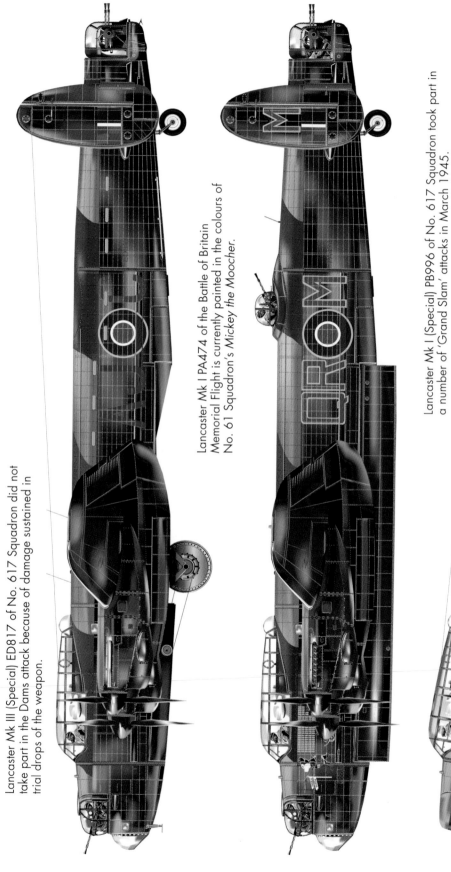

Lancaster Mk III (Special) ED817 of No. 617 Squadron did not take part in the Dams attack because of damage sustained in trial drops of the weapon.

Lancaster Mk I PA474 of the Battle of Britain Memorial Flight is currently painted in the colours of No. 61 Squadron's *Mickey the Moocher*.

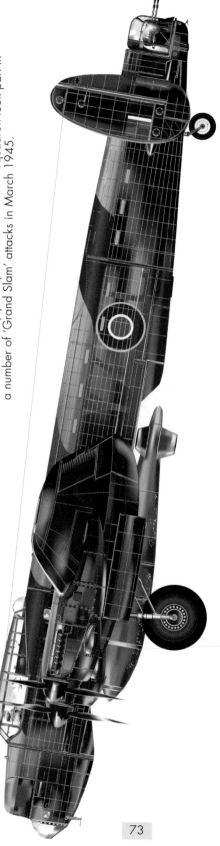

Lancaster Mk I (Special) PB996 of No. 617 Squadron took part in a number of 'Grand Slam' attacks in March 1945.

designation was later changed to MP for maritime patrol duties.

Lancaster Mk 10N: Three aircraft were converted to flying classrooms for trainee navigators.

Lancaster Mk 10O: A flying test-bed with two Avro (Canada) Orenda turbojets mounted in the outer engine nacelles.

Lancaster Mk 10P: Nine aircraft were modified for photographic reconnaissance and mapping duties.

Lancaster Mk 10S: The designation 'Standard' was allocated to Lancasters for museum or display purposes and also to aircraft held in storage which were used to supply spares for active aircraft.

Lancaster Mk 10SR: Eight aircraft were converted for air-sea rescue duties.

Lancaster Mk 10U: Aircraft held in storage which were unmodified for any specific role. Replacement aircraft could be drawn from this stock and converted as necessary.

Lancaster XPP: Civilian designation allocated to the six aircraft for Trans Canada Airlines.

France: Between December 1951 and February 1954 the Aéronavale received 54 Lancasters, including 32 Mk Is and 22 Mk VIIs. With the designation Western Union (WU) the aircraft were purchased at a cost of £50,000 each in a North Atlantic Treaty Organisation (NATO) agreement. These aircraft mainly served on maritime reconnaissance duties operating from the French colonies in the South Pacific. Five Lancaster Mk VIIs were purchased by the French Government for ASR duties. Although classed as a civilian purchase these aircraft, mainly based in

When this shot was taken in May 1945, Champagne Charlie was CF-C² of No. 625 Squadron with 12 operations marked. The aircraft then became ZN-K of No. 106 Squadron at Metheringham. In November 1945 NN757 joined the hundreds of other aircraft at No. 20 MU and was scrapped in May 1947.

Algeria and Morocco, were flown by French Navy crews.

Argentina: The Argentine air force received 15 Lancaster Mk Is with deliveries commencing in May 1948 continuing until January 1949. The aircraft were taken out of storage, slightly modified and delivered from the Avro facility at Langar, Nottinghamshire. The aircraft served in bomber units with duties including border patrols and reconnaissance. They saw action during the revolutionary period of the 1950s. At least two were converted to long-range transports and, barring accidents, most of the Lancasters remained into the 1960s.

Egypt: At the end of June 1950, the Royal Egyptian Air Force took delivery of the first of nine Lancaster Mk Is from Avro at Bracebridge Heath, Lincoln. The aircraft seemed to be little used and it is possible that they were scrapped or destroyed in one of Egypt's clashes with Israel, but whatever the answer the Lancasters disappeared completely.

Sweden: The Royal Swedish Air Force ordered a Lancaster to act as a test-bed for the Stal Dovern turbojet engine programme. A Mk I was taken from storage at No. 46 MU at Lossiemouth to be converted by Air Service Training at Hamble with delivery being made on 24 April 1951. The large test installation was mounted under the centre fuselage, with tests on engines and afterburners being carried out in Sweden during the early 1950s. It was on one of these test flights on 8 May 1956 that a serious fire in the port outer Merlin engine caused the aircraft to crash and be destroyed.

Right: The RAF Battle of Britain Memorial Flight's Lancaster is currently painted to represent *Mickey the Moocher*, but this photograph shows the real wartime aircraft after 83 operations while serving as OF-N and OF-O with No. 97 Squadron and then QR-M of No. 61 Squadron. *Mickey* flew its first operational mission with No. 97 on 3/4 July 1943, when it joined a raid against Cologne, and subsequently went on to serve with No. 61 Squadron on 20 September 1943. Its maiden flight from Woodford was on 2 June 1943, in the capable hands of Bill Thorn and just nine days later EE176 arrived at Oakington to serve with No. 7 Squadron. It was transferred to No. 97 Squadron on 21 June, but it was for its service with No. 61 that the aircraft will be remembered. Although varying totals for the number of operations completed are quoted, with 115 perhaps being recorded on the nose and as many as 128 suggested by some historians, it is generally assumed that the total was 122.

Lancaster Mk II DS842 JI-F of No. 514 Squadron and *Fanny Firkin II*, caused some excitement after landing at the US 8th Air Force base at Deenethorpe on 20 February 1944. The base was home to the the 401st Bomb Group's B-17s and the Americans were dismayed at the size of the Lancaster's bomb bay. DS842 ended its days with No. 1668 Heavy Conversion Unit (HCU) at Bottesford before being declared surplus on 20 March 1945.

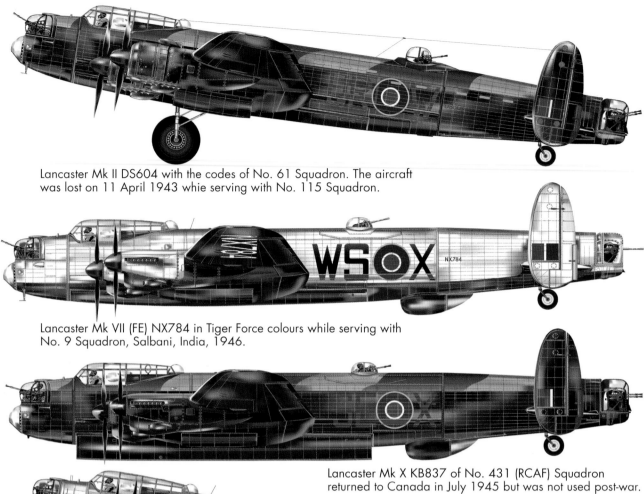

Lancaster Mk II DS604 with the codes of No. 61 Squadron. The aircraft was lost on 11 April 1943 whie serving with No. 115 Squadron.

Lancaster Mk VII (FE) NX784 in Tiger Force colours while serving with No. 9 Squadron, Salbani, India, 1946.

Lancaster Mk X KB837 of No. 431 (RCAF) Squadron returned to Canada in July 1945 but was not used post-war.

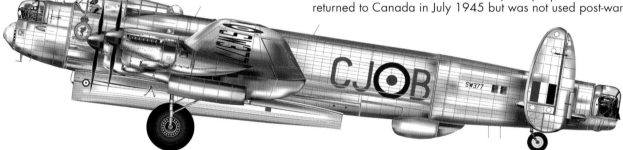

Lancaster ASR/GR.Mk III SW377 carried a lifeboat while operated by No. 203 Squadron at St Eval, Cornwall, in 1947.

Lancaster Mk VII (Western Union) WU-13 of the French Aéronavale was formerly NX665. The aircraft is now preserved in New Zealand in RAF colours.

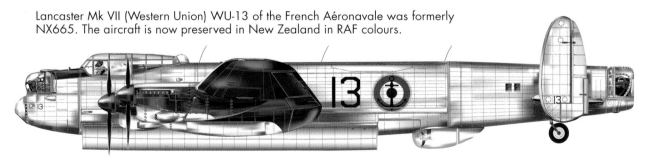

Lancaster Mk VII (Western Union) WU-15 is now *Just Jane* at East Kirkby.

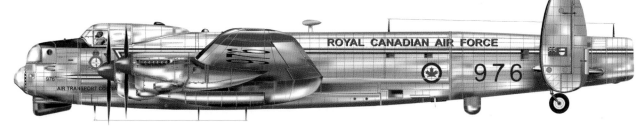

Lancaster Mk 10AR KB979 of No. 408 (RCAF) Squadron. The aircraft's war service was as LQ-K with No. 405 (RCAF) Squadron. it is currently being restored in the USA.

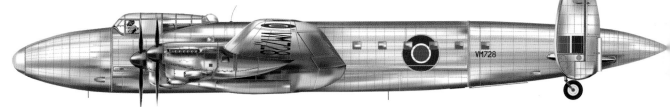

Lancaster VM728 was allocated civil registration G-AGMV but this was not used. It went to Rolls-Royce for engine trials in April 1947. It was scrapped in 1950.

Lancaster Mk II LL735 employed on gas-turbine engine development flying. Metro-Vick F.2/4A in tail.

Lancaster Mk I PA474 while serving at the College of Aeronautics, Cranfield, for laminar-flow aerofoil trials. It is now more famous as the BBMF's Lancaster.

Right: With the individual aircraft letter 'N' being relatively common, it is not surprising that there were a number of *Naughty Nans* in the RAF, with this example being Lancaster Mk III DV161 WS-N of No. 9 Squadron. The aircraft served with a number of squadrons, but was destroyed in a crash soon after take-off from North Luffenham on 16 January 1945, while operating with No. 1653 HCU.

Right: In this magnificent piece of Lancaster nose art, *Fannin' Fanny* on NX554, an Austin-built machine which joined No. 427 (RCAF) Squadron as ZL-F in March 1945, the unit must have had the finest artwork in Bomber Command. The bomber was transferred to No. 424 (RCAF) Squadron just as that unit disbanded, immediately going into storage at Aston Down with No. 20 MU. After almost a year parked-up, NX554 was Struck off Charge on 23 October 1946.

Left: After being delivered to No. 103 Squadron in March 1943, ED731 was given the code-letters PM-A and the name *Dante's Daughter*. It retained the name when it was transferred to No. 166 Squadron as AS-T^2. It is seen here receiving its 65th operation marker, but was unfortunately shot down on the homeward leg after bombing Berlin on the night of 24/25 March 1944, with the codes AS-Q.

Left: *Press On Regardless*, the unofficial motto of Bomber Command, was painted under the cockpit of ED905 *Ad Extremum* which completed its 100th operation on 2 November 1944. Commencing its career in April 1943 as PM-X with No. 103 Squadron, the aircraft then went to the newly formed No. 166 Squadron as AS-X. After a major overhaul, ED905 was allocated to No. 550 Squadron becoming BQ-F. While with No. 103, the aircraft had a Belgian pilot and its nose art consisted of crossed flags of the Union Jack and Belgium, but after the overhaul and repaint in June 1944 it received the *Ad Extremum* crest. After retirement ED905 went on to No. 1656 HCU via No. 1 LFS, before being damaged beyond repair after swinging off the runway while landing at Lindholme on 20 August 1945. This photograph shows the Lancaster after its 70th operation with its skipper, David Shaw, in the cockpit.

Appendix 1. Specifications and Performance

Production Mk I

Crew:
Pilot: captain of the aircraft regardless of rank
Flight engineer: normally trained by the pilot to fly the aircraft straight and level
Navigator
Bomb aimer: Later called bombardier in US style. Also operated the front gun turret
Wireless operator
Mid-upper gunner
Rear gunner
Special wireless operator: used on No. 101 Squadron aircraft to operate ABC equipment

Dimensions: length 69 ft 6 in; height 20 ft 6 in; wing span 102 ft; wing chord at root 16 ft; wing chord at tip joint 9 ft 2 in, aileron span 17 ft 3 in; aileron mean chord 2 ft 6 in; tailplane span 33 ft; tailplane mean chord 7 ft; wing area 1,297 sq ft; tailplane area 237 sq ft; fins and rudders area 111.4 sq ft
Performance: maximum speeds 287 mph at 11,500 ft, 275 mph at 15,000 ft, 260 mph at 19,400 ft; cruising speeds 234 mph at 21,000 ft,

Table showing increased Lancaster weights and other parameters by mark.

Date Type	January 1942 Production Mk I	September 1942 Production Mk II	November 1942 Production Mk I	May 1944 Mk I/III	Early 1945 Mk I/III overload
Structure	17,064 lb	17,064 lb	17,776 lb	18,033 lb	17,633 lb
Powerplant	10,720 lb	12,335 lb	11,304 lb	11,610 lb	11,610 lb
Fuel and oil tanks	1,796 lb	1,796 lb	1,999 lb	1,999 lb	1,999 lb
Empty weight	29,580 lb	31,195 lb	31,070 lb	31,642 lb	31,242 lb
Fixed military load	4,120 lb	4,120 lb	4,334 lb	5,169 lb	4,589 lb
Tare weight	33,700 lb	35,315 lb	35,404 lb	36,811 lb	35,831 lb
Crew, removable military load, fuel and oil, bombs and carriers	26,300 lb	24,685 lb	27,596 lb	28,189 lb	36,169 lb
Gross weight	60,000 lb	60,000 lb	63,000 lb	65,000 lb	72,000 lb
Take-off power	5,120 bhp	6,200 bhp	5,120 bhp	6,440 bhp	6,440 bhp
Wing loading	46.26 lb/sq ft	46.26 lb/sq ft	48.57 lb/sq ft	50.12 lb/sq ft	55.51 lb/sq ft
Span loading	5.77 lb/sq ft	5.77 lb/sq ft	6.06 lb/sq ft	6.25 lb/sq ft	6.92 lb/sq ft
Power loading (take-off power)	11.72 lb/bhp	9.68 lb/bhp	12.30 lb/bhp	10.09 lb/bhp	11.18 lb/bhp

200 mph at 15,000 ft; stalling speed (clean) 95 mph at 60,000 lb; maximum diving speed 360 mph; rate of climb 250 ft per minute; service ceiling 23,000 ft; absolute ceiling 24,500 ft; range 2,530 miles with 7,000 lb bomb load, 1,730 miles with 12,000 lb bomb, 1,550 miles with 22,000 lb bomb

Maximum take-off weight: 63,000 lb in November 1942; 65,000 lb in May 1944; 72,000 lb in February 1945

Maximum fuel load: 2,154 Imp gal

Powerplants
Prototype: Rolls-Royce Merlin X (1,145 hp)
Mk I: Rolls-Royce Merlin XX, 22 or 24 (1,280 hp/ 1,620 hp)
Mk I (Special): Rolls-Royce Merlin 22 or 24 (1,280 hp/1,620 hp)
Mk II: Bristol Hercules VI or XVI (1,650 hp)
Mk III: Packard Merlin 28 (1,300 hp), or Packard-Merlin 38 (1,390 hp), or Packard-Merlin 224 (1,640 hp)
Mk VI: Rolls-Royce Merlin 85 (1,750 hp)
Mk VII: Rolls-Royce Merlin 24 (1,620 hp)
Mk X: Packard Merlin 28 (1,300 hp), or 38 (1,390 hp), or 224 (1,640 hp)

The Repeater Compass is shown in this shot of Pilot Officer Jim Cowan, RNZAF, and Flight Engineer Charlie Doswell in their No. 9 Squadron Lancaster at Waddington in September 1942.

The radio operator's station was on the port side, immediately aft of the navigator's table and as the nerve centre of the aircraft everything was at hand. The excellent radio equipment was the Marconi Transmitter T.1154 and Receiver R.1155 with a Morse key on the right of the radio man's table. The operator was also provided with a switching gear to connect crew positions to the receiver or transmitter if required.

Propellers
Rotol, Hamilton-Standard or the paddle-bladed Nash-Kelvinator were used. The latter improved cruising speed by approximately 8 mph and service ceiling by 1,500 ft.

Rolls-Royce Merlin engine data
Engine type: 12-cylinder poppet valve upright Vee, pressure liquid cooled
Bore: 5.4 in
Stroke: 6 in
Compression ratio: 6:1
Swept volume: 27.01 litre (1,649 cu in)

This Lancaster cockpit layout shows the standard blind flying panel to the left, with the eight ignition switches above the instruments for the four engines. To the top right are the engine starting buttons over the propeller feathering switches and the fire extinguisher buttons. Out of the picture in the centre console are the four throttle levers and propeller speed controls and to the rear of the console was the trim wheel and undercarriage selection lever. This is the cockpit of the first production aircraft.

Supercharger:
Type: mechanically driven, two-speed, single stage, centrifugal
Gear ratios: 8.15:1 and 9.49:1
Rotor diameter: 10.25 in

Airscrew shaft: SBAC No. 5
Airscrew reduction gear ratio: 0.42:1
Direction of rotation:
Airscrew shaft: right-hand tractor
Crankshaft: left-hand

Ignition: two magnetos BTH C.5 SE12-S or Rotax NSE12-4
Starting: electric starter motor
Air intake: updraught

Carburation: SU float carburettor, type AVT 40/214/216/224/227
Fuel specification: 100/130 Grade DED 2475 (AN-F-28)
Specific gravity at 15°C: 0.71–0.73
Oil specification: DED 2472/B/O
Coolant specification: 70 per cent water + 30 per cent ethylene glycol to specification DTD 344 A
Coolant capacity of engine (bare): 5 Imp gal

Weight of engine, nett dry: Mark XX and 21 1,450 lb; Mark 22 and 23 1,455 lb; Mark 24 and 25 1,470 lb; Mark T. 24-2 1,540 lb; Mark T.24-4 1,575 lb

Centre of gravity:
Above crankshaft centreline: 4.0–5.6 in

This view of the centre of the instrument panel shows additional instruments on the top of the coaming, with the Direction Finding Indicator and Repeater Compass as fitted to later Lancasters.

Aft of cylinder block centreline: 4.58–5.025 in
To right of crankshaft centreline: 0.05 – 0.40 in

Specific gravity, estimated, including coolant and oil: 2.55

Lancaster facts

The average cost per aircraft was £58,974 which included airframe, engines, propellers and flight systems, but not government equipment such as guns, radio, radar and bombsight. The total number of items in the aircraft was 120,000.

The number of jigs and tools required to build a Lancaster was 25,000.

The number of construction drawings totalled 10,500.

Each aircraft had over seven miles of electrical cable.

Six months of Lancaster production required

enough light alloy sheet and strip to cover a roadway 30 ft wide from Manchester to London.

During Wings for Victory Week in 1943, the Lancasters on display were L7580 of No. 207 Squadron in London, the new ED749 in Manchester and No. 97 Squadron's R5552 in Leeds. It seemed appropriate that the city of Lancaster should host the new ED999. Collections held in that week raised £7,206,157.

This rare photograph shows one of the Lancaster Mk VIs in squadron service. This aircraft is JB713 as LQ-P with No. 405 (RCAF) Squadron at Gransden Lodge. The machine then joined No. 635 Squadron as F2-Z, but was shot down while attacking Harburg on the night of 18/19 August 1944. The Merlin 85s have their engines covered, but the bomb aimer's blister shows the two small rings which were known as the 'Z' equipment for identification friend or foe (IFF).

Appendix 2. Weapons and Systems

The role of any bomber aircraft is to deliver a load of bombs to a specified target, but it also must be able to defend itself during such an operation.

The Lancaster's defensive armament evolved from the experience gained from operations of bombers earlier in the war including the Wellington, the Stirling and in particular the Avro Manchester.

Defensive armament: Nose turret

The Frazer-Nash FN 5 turret, designed in 1938

Below: The Frazer-Nash FN 5 front turret became the standard fit on Lancasters throughout the war, after proving its worth on both the Manchester and Wellington – it was originally designed for the latter. Slightly modified for use on the Lancaster, the turret was designated Type 5A and equipped with two 0.303-in Brownings. Its capacity was 1,000 rounds per gun.

for the Wellington, became standard for the RAF's heavy bombers including the Manchester and the design of the Lancaster required only a slightly improved version known as the FN Type 5A. The turret was fitted with two 0.303-in Browning machine-guns, each fed by 1,000 rounds. The hydraulically operated turret was normally manned by the bomb aimer and could be rotated by hand in the event of a systems

Above: The mid-upper turret for the majority of Lancasters was the FN 50, also fitted with two 0.303-in Browning machine-guns, each with 1,000 rounds and with a full 360° line of fire. As illustrated on KB839, a Mk X serving with No. 419 (RCAF) Squadron as KR-D, the fairing around the turret incorporated a cam track which prevented the guns damaging any part of the aircraft. An improved version was known as the FN 150 and Martin turrets equipped with two 0.5-in Brownings were fitted to the Mk VII and Canadian-built Mk X aircraft.

failure. This turret remained a feature of all Lancaster versions throughout the war with the exception of the Mk I (Special) when it was deleted to save weight.

Mid-upper turret

Replacing the Frazer-Nash FN 7 turret on the Avro Manchester was the FN 50, also armed with two 0.303-in Brownings with the same rounds capacity as the nose turret. With a full 360° line of fire, with elevation and depression, the possibility of damaging areas of the aircraft was eliminated in March 1942 when this turret

was fitted with a fairing which incorporated a cam track to guide the gun fire away from causing harm. A later version known as the FN 150 was fitted to production Lancasters from the middle of 1944, this turret having improved sighting and gun control mechanisms. The Martin Type 250 turret equipped with twin 0.5-in Browning machine-guns equipped the Austin-built Lancaster Mk VII after trials by A&AEE. This turret was positioned further forward than normal and took up too much space in the aircraft to the irritation of the crews. Trials were also undertaken with the Bristol B17 turret which was later fitted to the Avro Lincoln. The licence-built French Hispano 20-mm cannon fitted in remote-controlled barbettes was tested on a Lancaster after the war.

Ventral turret

The ventral turret consisted of a Frazer-Nash FN 64 fitted with two 0.303-in guns with the turret being faired into the rear of the bulged bomb bay doors. However, it was not popular with some units and in many cases it was removed completely as with Nos 1 and 5 Groups. The loss of many bombers in unknown circumstances proved to be a mystery until it was discovered that the Luftwaffe night fighters were using upward firing cannon known as *Schräge Musik*. The German aircraft would approach underneath in the bomber's blind spot before firing upwards into the machine's fuel tanks. Having set the bomber ablaze, the fighter would bank away quickly to avoid colliding with the falling bomber or any damage should the victim explode. A number of bomber squadrons attempted to combat these attacks by fitting a free-mounted 0.5-in Browning attached to the rear of the bomb bay. The gunner sat on a bicycle-type seat with a box of ammunition being bolted to the floor of the bomb compartment. A large panel was removed from

This is the FN 82 turret, fitted with two 0.5-in Brownings, designed to replace the standard FN 20 which was the most widely used of the Lancaster tail turrets. The FN 20 had the four 0.303-in guns and was updated to improved FN 120 standard. Another tail turret, developed by Rose Brothers, was much roomier and carried two 0.5-in guns, but was only used by No. 1 Group from mid-1944.

This impressive-looking installation is built around an FN 121 turret with the dome housing a radar scanner for the AGL(T) 'Village Inn' gun laying equipment. The aerial above the turret gave warning of an approaching Luftwaffe night fighter using FuG 202/212 transmissions. It also alerted the Lancaster's crew that one of the giant *Würzburg* radars was plotting their course.

the fuselage floor with the gun being fired through the aperture. In the Lancaster's early life a little known project was to mount a hand-operated Vickers K-type 0.303-in gun in the ventral position.

Tail turret

The Frazer-Nash FN 20 turret fitted with four 0.303-in Brownings covered the rear of the Lancaster with 2,500 rounds per gun fed by belts from ammunition boxes mounted in the rear fuselage. In May 1943 this type started to be replaced by the FN 120 with a greatly improved heating system. This, in turn, was updated as the FN 121 to be equipped with 'Village Inn' which was the code-name for the Automatic Gun Laying AGL(T) radar sighting system. The Rose Brothers company of Gainsborough development a rear turret much roomier than the FN types with this carrying two 0.5-in Browning machine-guns, while another Frazer-Nash type was the later FN 82 which was also fitted with twin 0.5-in guns and equipped the Lancaster Mk VII.

Gun sighting

Optical specialists Barr & Stroud developed the G.III gun sight which was the standard equipment on British bombers for most of the war. The reflector sight projected an orange aiming reticle, which was focused to infinity, onto a glass screen with the brightness being controlled by the gunner during either night or daytime. The screen, mounted at 45°, consisted of a circle image with a centre spot, with this being the equivalent of an enemy aircraft at 400 yards. Later in the war gyroscopic gun sights equipped most bombers while the radar sighting AGL(T) was fitted with an infra-red detector to prevent friendly aircraft closing from behind from being shot down. Two infra-red lamps were located in the nose blister of Lancasters to give warning to the AGL(T) of the aircraft ahead. This was known as the Z-system.

Typical Lancaster bomb loads

Bomb Type	Abbreviation
Armour Piercing	AP
Anti-Shipping	AS
Deep Penetration	DP
General Purpose	GP
High Capacity	HC
High Explosive	HE
Light Case	LC
Medium Capacity	MC
Research Department Explosives	RDX
Semi-Armour Piercing	SAP
Small Bomb Container	SBC
Capital Ship	CS

Mining operations: six 1,850-lb parachute mines which could be of the acoustic or magnetic type. First used on the type's operational debut on the night of 3/4 March 1942.

Industrial area bombing: targets including marshalling yards, shipyards and factories required a typical load of 14 1,000-lb GP or MC bombs. These could be delayed action or instantaneous detonation type, or a mixture.

Area bombing – Incendiary and Blast: one 4,000-lb 'Cookie', plus 12 Small Bomb Containers (SBC) each carrying either 236 of the 4-lb type incendiary or 24 of the 30-lb variety.

Area bombing – Fire and Blast: this mixed load would consist of one 4,000-lb bomb with impact fuse, three 1,000-lb HE bombs and six SBCs with incendiaries.

Area bombing – Demolition and Blast: this load was used on heavily industrialised target areas and contained one 8,000-lb HC bomb, and six 500-lb MC or GP type bombs.

Area bombing – Incendiary: this maximum fire load had 14 SBCs carrying incendiaries. The average load would be 14,000 lb.

Low-level bombing: usually this operation was carried out using six 1,000-lb GP or MC type bombs with delay fuses of various timings to suit the mission requirement.

Tactical targets – Carpet Bombing: one 4,000-lb bomb fitted with impact fuse, plus 18 500-lb GP or MC bombs with mixed fusing. This type of load was used to support the Allied ground forces after the invasion, and was also used against V-weapon launching sites.

The 'Tallboy': carried in Lancasters with bulged bomb doors, this 12,000-lb, spin-stabilised, deep penetration bomb was used against German U-boat pens, the giant battleship *Tirpitz* and other heavily fortified targets. From June 1944 until hostilities ceased 854 'Tallboys' were used.

The Grand Slam: this massive weapon was carried exclusively by the Lancaster (Special) which had its bomb doors removed to accommodate the 22,000-lb bomb. The nose and mid-upper gun turrets were also removed to save weight and a strengthened undercarriage was fitted in the event that the aircraft had to return to base with this type of bomb still on board. Altogether 41 Grand Slams were used on operations with the first being dropped against the Bielefeld railway viaduct on 14 March 1945.

Bomb loads

Throughout the war the average bomb load for the Lancaster was 14,000 lb with many combinations being available depending on the type of operation or range required, using the weapons described in this Appendix.

Bomb sights
Mark IXA Course-Setting Bomb Sight (CSBS)
Mark XIV Computing Bomb Site (CBS)

Camera
An F.24 camera was standard equipment for vertical photography to confirm bombing accuracy.

Appendix 3. Production Details

The Lancaster Production Group
The Lancaster Production Group was formed in September 1941 with its organisation based on the experience gained from production of the Avro Manchester.

The nucleus of that Group consisted of A.V. Roe & Company Limited, the parent design firm, plus Metropolitan-Vickers and, later, these were joined by Armstrong Whitworth and Fairey Aviation. The latter subsequently left the Group owing to the reduction in production requirements. In 1941 the Lancaster Group consisted of Avro, Metropolitan-Vickers, Armstrong Whitworth and Vickers-Armstrong of Castle Bromwich. In March 1943 the Group was further expanded to meet the increasing demand for Lancasters with Vickers-Armstrong, Chester and the Austin Motor Company of Birmingham, becoming members.

Victory Aircraft Limited was established at Malton, Toronto, Canada specifically to produce the Lancaster Mk X. Deliveries from Canada commenced in September 1943 with two batches totalling 430 aircraft being built by May 1945.

Messrs Short & Harland of Belfast were also intending to become members of the Group, commencing with an order for 200 Lancasters, but this was later cancelled as it was found that the whole production requirements could be satisfied by the existing Group.

Development of the Lanaster
As Lancaster production was proceeding the parent firm was actively engaged in the development and manufacturing planning of a Super Lancaster which eventually became known as the Avro Lincoln. The European war was drawing to a close as this aircraft was coming into production, but it had already been decided to reduce the Group to just three with Avro, Armstrong Whitworth and Metropolitan-Vickers staying together for production of the Lincoln. However, with the conclusion of the war against the Japanese, Metropolitan-Vickers left the Group. Vickers-Armstrong at Castle Bromwich and Chester, along with Austin Motors, had already completed their Lancaster production contracts, but it was not until 5 December 1945 that the Avro Lancaster Production Group was formally wound up at Claridges Hotel, London.

The contractors
A.V. Roe & Company Limited
Managing Director: Sir Roy Dobson
Assistant General Manager and Director: Mr C.E. Fielding
General Manager: Mr J. Green
Chief Superintendent: Mr J.A.R. Kay (Secretary of the Group)

The parent company completed its first production Lancaster in October 1941 with its last in October 1945, during which period the production rate reached a peak of 155 aircraft per month in August 1944. The Avro manufacturing totals include Chadderton and Yeadon. Avro Chadderton produced the major components with the assembly and flight testing being undertaken at Woodford. The Yeadon factory, which is on the site of the now Leeds-Bradford Airport, manufactured and test flew the aircraft.

The totals for both sides:

Chadderton: Mk I   842
               Mk III   2,133
               Total   2,975   (plus   three
prototypes)

Yeadon: Mk I   54
               Mk III   641
               Total   695

Overall total: 3,670 (plus prototypes)

The Woodford contribution in the assembly and flight testing of the Lancaster was 4,040 with the best week of production coming in June 1944 when 56 were delivered. In the production hall, known as New Assembly, the production racks were each one quarter of a mile long with two of these being devoted to Chadderton production (2,975) while a third track was for the assembly of Metropolitan-Vickers aircraft coming from Trafford Park, Manchester (1,065). The latter's last 15 aircraft were taken to Chester for assembly and flight test.

Metropolitan-Vickers Limited, Trafford Park, Manchester
General Manager & Director: Mr T. Fraser
Works Manager: Mr A.J. Leslie

The first aircraft was delivered to Woodford for assembly in January 1942, with the last being in August 1945. The last 15 Lancasters were completed at Chester. During the manufacturing period the company reached a peak of 45 machines per month in August 1944.

Production: Mk I   944

Mk III   136
Total   1,080

Austin Aero Limited, Longbridge, Birmingham
Manager: Mr F.V. Smith
Production Manager: Mr G.A. Durant

The Austin firm produced its first Lancaster in March 1944 and was still producing aircraft late into 1945. A peak of 35 machines per month was achieved in June 1945. The completed aircraft total was not as originally planned, but with the termination of the war the contract was reduced as it was envisaged that production would continue until June 1946.

Production: Mk I   150
               Mk VII   180
               Total   330

Vickers-Armstrong Limited, Castle Bromwich
Lancaster Production Director: Mr W.A. Dixon

The first production batch of Lancasters was ordered on 30 September 1942 with the original contract calling for 200 of the radial-engined Mk II. The contract was revised to the Mk III on 13 February 1943, but on 28 April 1943 the order was changed once again, this time to the Mk I as only British-built Merlin engines were being delivered to Castle Bromwich. Deliveries for the first batch commenced in November 1943 and continued until February 1945 with a further batch of 100 taking production through to August 1945. December 1944 was the best month with 25 Lancasters delivered.

Production: Mk I   300

Vickers-Armstrong Limited, Chester
Superintendent: Mr B.A. Duncan
Sub-Contracts Manager: Mr Lefevre

Although most of the Lancaster work was sub-contracted, final assembly was carried out at Hawarden, Chester. The plant's first Lancaster appeared in June 1944 and after reaching a peak of 36 aircraft in March 1945 production ended in the following September. It must be noted that the last 15 Lancasters produced by Metropolitan-Vickers in Manchester were transported to Chester for completion between June and August 1945. These aircraft, of course, appear in the Metro-Vick production total.

Production: Mk I   235

Sir W.G. Armstrong Whitworth Aircraft Limited, Coventry (AWA)
General Manager and Director: Mr W. Woodhams
Assistant General Manager: Mr P.G. Crabbe
Works Manager: Mr E.L. Lockwood

As a sister company to Avro within the Hawker Siddeley Group and one of the original members of the Lancaster consortium, Armstrong Whitworth produced the largest number of Lancasters next to the parent company. Its first Lancasters rolled off the production line in August 1942 continuing until October 1945, with an excellent 75 machines per month in October 1944. AWA was the only one of the Lancaster Production Group to produce the radial-engined Mk II.

Production: Mk I   919
                Mk II   300
                Mk III   110
                Total   1,329

Victory Aircraft Limited, Malton, Toronto, Canada
Avro Representative: Mr Alfred Sewart

Under the guidance of Avro Managing Director Roy (later Sir Roy) Dobson, Victory Aircraft Limited was established specifically to build the Avro Lancaster. The Canadian version, known as the Mk X (ten) was equipped with the American-built Packard Merlin engine. The first production contract was for 300 aircraft with the first aircraft arriving in England for evaluation late in September 1943. A second production batch of 200 aircraft was ordered, but this contract was terminated at the end of the war after 130 had been built. The best months were April/May 1945 when 35 Lancasters were delivered.

Production   Mk X   430

Production record

The Lancaster Production Group had a wartime record for which it can be extremely proud. After the three prototypes the Group delivered a total of 7,374 Lancasters. It is also estimated that, in the various components built for the Avro Repair Units to replace either battle-damaged or crash-damaged parts, enough spares were manufactured to have completed another 622 Lancasters!

At the parent company Avro, with sites at Chadderton, Woodford and Yeadon plus many smaller units, a total of 29,600 were employed at its peak. A further 1,100 were engaged in Repair Units which were based at the Avro facilities at Bracebridge Heath, Lincolnshire and Langar, Nottinghamshire. Each station operating the Lancaster would also have an Avro representative on site. It is of note that 46 of the manufacturing workers were female.

Production summary

Contractor	Mark	Contract
Avro Manchester/Yeadon	I	896
Avro Manchester/Yeadon	III	2,774
Metropolitan-Vickers	I	944
Metropolitan-Vickers	III	136
Austin Motors Limited	I	150
Austin Motors Limited	VII	180
Vickers-Armstrongs (C.B.)	I	300
Vickers-Armstrongs (Chester)	I	235
Armstrong Whitworth	I	919
Armstrong Whitworth	II	300
Armstrong Whitworth	III	110
Victory Aircraft, Canada	X	430
Avro Prototypes		3
Total		**7,377**

Note: Avro Manchester includes Chadderton & Woodford.
The eight Lancaster Mk VI aircraft were converted from Mk IIIs.

Total by mark:

Prototypes	3
Mk I	3,444
Mk II	300
Mk III	3,020
Mk VII	180
Mk X	430
Total	**7,377**

Appendix 4. Museum Aircraft and Warbirds

UNITED KINGDOM

Mk I, R5868

Preserved in the RAF Museum at Hendon, this famous Lancaster completed 137 operations while serving with No. 83 Squadron as OL-Q and 467 Squadron as PO-S. Painted in the colours of the latter, the aircraft has the inscription, *No Enemy Plane will fly over the Reich Territory*, the well-known quote from Hermann Goering.

Mk I, W4964

The rear fuselage and other parts of this aircraft, which completed 106 operations while serving as WS-J with No. 9 Squadron, are on display at Newark Air Museum, Winthorpe, Nottingham. The aircraft bears the title *Johnny Walker – Still Going Strong* after the famous brand of whisky.

Mk I, DV373

The complete nose and cockpit section of this aircraft are displayed in London's Imperial War Museum. After service with No. 467 Squadron as PO-F, the aircraft was badly damaged in a landing accident on 4 October 1945 and Struck off Charge.

Mk VII, NX611

Just Jane of the Lincolnshire Aviation Heritage Centre at East Kirkby now wears the markings of Nos 57 and 630 Squadrons which were based at that airfield for their wartime operations. This Austin-built Mk VII did not see service until it was delivered as WU-15 to the French Navy in

May 1952. In 1965 the machine was donated to the UK-based Historic Aircraft Preservation Society (HAPS) and registered G-ASXX. After a checkered period, thankfully it was purchased by Fred and Harold Panton in memory of their brother who lost his life on operations while serving in a Lancaster. This aircraft is an excellent representation of a wartime Lancaster and is taxied at regular intervals. The machine has featured in a number of TV shows devoted to the Lancaster.

Mk I, PA474

Operated by the RAF's Battle of Britain Memorial Flight (BBMF) from the wartime Lancaster base at Coningsby, Lincolnshire, this aircraft still flies regularly at air shows and various ceremonial events. The Chester-built machine was completed in August 1945 and was stored until delivered to No. 82 Squadron as a PR.Mk I for photographic reconnaissance duties on 21 September 1948. In August 1952 it was allocated to Flight Refuelling Limited at Tarrant Rushton, but was unused by that company and transferred to the College of Aeronautics at Cranfield where it was engaged in flight-testing various aerofoil sections mounted on top of the fuselage. After some excellent work, the Lancaster was returned to the RAF and wisely passed to the Air Historical Branch for preservation. After a period of storage the aircraft was flown to Waddington into the care of No. 44 Squadron from August 1965 until it was transferred to the BBMF in November 1973. Thankfully, PA474 receives regular overhauls

This 1973 photograph of PA474 *City of Lincoln* shows the aircraft in the code letters of the machine in which John Nettleton won his VC on 17 April 1942. PA474 did not see service in the war, and first appeared in wartime camouflage in 1966 after being restored by the RAF at Henlow. Since that time the machine has worn the codes of a number of famous Lancasters. As a PR.Mk I nose, tail and mid-upper turrets had to be added, but after receiving the aircraft from the College of Aeronautics in 1964, the RAF steadily modified PA474 to the excellent condition it is in today with the Battle of Britain Memorial Flight at RAF Coningsby, where it is lovingly cared for by a dedicated team. Sadly, the brave men who flew Lancasters are gradually fading away, but it is hoped that PA474 will continue to fly for many years to come, as a tribute to the wartime Bomber Command.

and in recent years the whole mainplane was completely rebuilt at the Chadderton factory of British Aerospace, the Lancaster's spiritual home. The aircraft's code-letters are changed during the overhaul period to represent famous Lancasters and with the flight's superb maintenance programme this aircraft will thrill the crowds for many years to come. The machine was originally named *City of Lincoln*.

Mk X, KB889
After eight years of restoration, this Canadian-built example was unveiled at the Imperial War Museum, Duxford, on 1 November 1994. It is now preserved in its wartime colours as NA-I of No. 428 Squadron at Middleton St George, where it arrived on 8 April 1945, but did not take part in any operations. Returning to Canada on 6 July 1945, the aircraft served as a Mk 10MP with No. 408 Squadron and No. 107 Rescue Unit. Declared

surplus in 1963, it was stored until purchased by Warbirds of Great Britain, appearing on the British Civil Register as G-LANC on 31 January 1985. However, the registration was cancelled on 2 September 1991 with the machine then being acquired by the Imperial War Museum.

Australia

Mk I, W4783
After completing 89 operations as AR-G with No. 460 Squadron, 'G-George' was retired from operations after returning from Cologne on 20 April 1944. The Royal Australian Air Force (RAAF) requested that the aircraft be allocated to the Australian War Memorial in Canberra and on 20 May 1944 W4783 was officially handed over to the RAAF during a ceremony at Binbrook, Lincolnshire. It was deemed that the aircraft was fit for the long flight to Australia and after

leaving Prestwick on 11 October 1944 the Lancaster arrived at Amberley, near Brisbane on 8 November 1944 – slightly longer than expected, but the delights of Canada, the USA and some of the Pacific islands were too good to miss! During March and April 1945 G-George completed a tour of Australia raising the magnificent total of £319,870 for the war effort. The aircraft made its final flight on 24 September 1945 from Laverton to Canberra and although given the Australian serial number A66-2 the Lancaster is now resplendent in its old wartime colours on display in the superb new ANZAC Hall of the Memorial facility.

Mk VII, NX622
Presented to the Royal Australian Air Force Association by the French Navy this aircraft is now in the RAAFA's Heritage Museum at Bull Creek, Perth, Western Australia. The machine did not see service with the RAF, being sold to the French in May 1952 and serving as WU-16 in Flottilles 24F, 25F and Escadrille 9S of the Aéronavale in the South Pacific, before being retired in December 1962. It is preserved in a Bomber Command-type colour scheme as LL847 JO-D of No. 463 Squadron.

New Zealand

Mk VII, NX665
Another of the Aéronavale gift aircraft was ex-WU-13 which, after a similar career to NX622, arrived in New Zealand to be displayed in the Museum of Transport, Technology and Social History in Auckland. It is painted as PB457 SR-V of No. 101 Squadron on the port side and as ND752 AA-O of the New Zealand No. 75 Squadron on the starboard.

France

Mk VII, NX664
The Pacific-based WU-21 had led a similar life to the other Aéronavale Lancasters before it was written-off in a crash on Wallis Island on 21 January 1963. The remains eventually returned to France where it is being rebuilt to exhibition standard by Ailes Anciennes at Le Bourget airport, Paris.

Canada

Mk X, FM104
Allocated to No. 428 Squadron at Middleton St George in April 1945, this aircraft returned to Canada on 13 August 1945. Converted to a Mk 10MR for service as CX104 with the RCAF, the machine was sold on 10 September 1964 and erected onto a plinth as RCAF Association memorial in the Canadian National Exhibition Grounds in Toronto.

Mk X, FM136
Followed a similar pattern to the Canadian-built Lancasters which were flown to England only to return to their homeland a few months later. This aircraft served as RX136, a Mk 10MR of No. 407 Squadron before being released to the Calgary Aerospace Museum on 10 April 1961. Restoration is currently in progress.

Mk X, FM159
Canadian service as Mk 10MR, RX159 of No. 407 Squadron. The aircraft also served with No. 103 Rescue Unit before being sold on 4 October 1960. Three residents of Nanton, Alberta, bought FM159 and after an excellent restoration it can now be seen in the Nanton Lancaster Society Air Museum, along with a fine collection of other types flown by the RCAF.

Mk X, FM212
Another Mk 10MR, this aircraft served for a short period as MN212 of No. 408 Squadron before going into storage. Sold on 10 October 1964, the Lancaster is now in Windsor, Ontario.

Mk X, FM213
After an extensive rebuild by the Canadian Warplane Heritage (CWH) Museum of Hamilton, Ontario, FM213 is now flying in the markings KB726 VR-A of No. 419 (RCAF) Squadron, the aircraft in which Pilot Officer Andrew Mynarski lost his life during an attack on Cambrai, France, on 12 June 1944. For outstanding bravery he was awarded the Victoria Cross (posthumously) and this aircraft flies as a tribute to this young Canadian who sacrificed his life trying to save a colleague. Lancaster FM213 was accepted by the RCAF on 21 August 1946, later serving with No. 405 Squadron and No. 107 Rescue Unit as

The world's second flying Lancaster is the Canadian Warplane Heritage aircraft painted in the colours of Andrew Mynarski's KB726 VR-A of No. 419 (RCAF) Squadron, which crashed on the night of 12/13 June 1944. The CWH aircraft is actually Lancaster Mk 10MR FM213, which has been magnificently restored by a team of volunteers with work commencing on 24 March 1983. The rebuild required many handmade parts and included Lincoln undercarriage legs and wheels fitted with Shackleton tyres. After the aircraft's first flight in 24 years, which took place on 11 September 1988, the Lancaster has performed regularly at air shows throughout Canada and in the United States. As with PA474, the Canadian Lancaster is a fine tribute to those who flew this wonderful aircraft.

CX213 and, with the latter, it was a frequent visitor to Britain during the early 1960s. Bought by the CWH on 30 June 1964, the aircraft was displayed statically. After restoration, the machine, now as KB726, took to the air again on 11 September 1988 in the capable hands of Squadron Leader Tony Banfield RAF, former CO of the BBMF. Alongside PA474, this aircraft is the only other flying Lancaster and is not only a fine tribute to Mynarski, but to all the other brave Canadians who flew operationally in a 'Lanc'.

Mk X, KB839

Seen at the Canadian Forces Base at Greenwood, Nova Scotia, this aircraft is one of the few surviving Lancasters to have seen action during the war. Arriving in England in January 1945, KB839 was allocated to No. 431 Squadron, but was soon transferred to No. 419, becoming VR-D and completing five operations before returning to Canada on 6 July 1945. Converted to a Mk 10AR it served with Nos 419 and 408 Squadrons before retirement.

Mk X, KB848

The nose section of this war veteran is on show at the National Aeronautical Collection, Rockcliffe, Ontario. As NA-G of No. 428 Squadron, the aircraft's first operation was to Dresden on 13/14 February 1945. After completing seven bombing raids the Lancaster returned to Canada on 6 June 1945 and went into storage. Modified as a Mk 10DC the aircraft was used to carry out trials with Ryan Firebee drones. The machine was sold for scrap on 3 April 1964. During the drone trials it wore the codes PX848.

Mk X, KB882

Another wartime aircraft of No. 428 Squadron was KB882 NA-R which was converted to a Mk 10MR after its return to Canada. After service with No. 408 Squadron as MN882, the Lancaster was up for disposal on 26 May 1964. It was flown to St Jacques airport, Edmunston, New Brunswick where it is displayed in its post-war colour scheme.

Mk X, KB944

The National Aeronautical Collection has this aircraft on show at Rockcliffe, Ontario. Originally with No. 425 Squadron in England as KW-K, the machine returned to Canada with the mass exodus of the Mk Xs at the end of the war. As a standard Mk 10 Lancaster it was with No. 404 Squadron until its retirement on 20 February 1957.

USA

Mk X, KB976

With No. 405 Squadron in England as LQ-K, this aircraft did not undertake any wartime operations before it was homeward bound on 28 June 1945. As a Mk 10AR the machine saw service with No. 408 Squadron as MN976 before being sold onto the Canadian civil register as CF-TQC on 6 June 1964 to be used as a water bomber. Purchased by Sir William Roberts it became G-BCOH, arriving at Auchterarder for the Strathallan Aircraft Collection on 20 May 1975, but was later sold to Charles Church Enterprises for rebuilding to flying condition. During its restoration the Lancaster suffered severe damage in a hangar collapse and following the death of the owner the aircraft was bought by the American collector Kermit Weeks of Polk City, Florida where the aircraft is in the process of being rebuilt using parts from Lancaster KB994.

Appendix 5. Model Kits

Model kits

Although the Lancaster is an extremely popular aircraft, the plastic model industry seems to have neglected the machine. Spitfires, Mustangs and the endless stream of Luftwaffe types represent the World War Two aircraft, while countless kits of fast jets cover the later generation. Many years ago a small-scale Lancaster was produced by Frog, but the kit was very basic and not too accurate, with Matchbox also manufacturing a 1:72nd scale kit. However, it is doubtful that either of these two are available except in model shops which specialise in selling the odd kit which is obsolete.

Airfix

Over 30 years ago Airfix produced an excellent 1:72nd scale Lancaster with markings to represent the famous W4783 'G-George' of No. 460 Squadron which is now on display in the Australian War Museum in Canberra. This kit was later revised into a Lancaster Mk III as ND458 HW-A of No. 100 Squadron named *Able Mabel* or with alternative markings supplied for ED888 PM-M[2] of No. 103 Squadron, both of which completed over 100 operations. In 1993 the kit appeared in 'Dambuster' form to mark the 50th Anniversary of the famous raid. The Airfix Lancaster is still available and can be built into an attractive model.

Tamiya

This Japanese kit manufacturer issued a Lancaster Mk I kit in 1:48th scale as long ago as 1975 and it is still an impressive kit even by today's standards. Excellent mouldings in black plastic and transparencies of a similarly high standard make the kit the finest available. The kit is a fine example of attention to detail and much can be achieved with interior painting, moveable control surfaces, opening bomb doors and, if required, a detailed Rolls-Royce Merlin in the starboard outer nacelle with a removable engine cowling. A comprehensive decal sheet allows the modeller three choices for the finished machine including WR118 ZN-Y *Admiral Prune* of No. 106 Squadron, ME545 XH-L *Lovely Lou* of No. 218 and the famous R5868 PO-S S-Sugar of No. 467 Squadron, as preserved in the RAF Museum at Hendon. As with the Airfix kit, a Dambuster version was released, but whichever is chosen the finished model will be superb.

Appendix 6. Further Reading

Avro Lancaster – The Definitive Record by Harry Holmes, Airlife 1997
Avro Lancaster – The Definitive Record (Second Edition), Airlife 2001
Lancaster – The Story of a Famous Bomber by Bruce Robertson, Harleyford 1964
Lancaster at War Vols 1–3 and 5 by Mike Garbett and Brian Goulding, Ian Allan 1971–1995
Lancaster at War Vol. 4 (Pathfinder Squadron) by Alex Thorne, Ian Allan 1990
Lancaster Bomber by D.B. Tubbs, Pan/Ballantine Books 1972
Lancaster in Action by Ron Mackay, Squadron/Signal Publications, USA, 1982
The Lancaster File by Jim Halley, Air Britain Publications 1985
The Avro Lancaster by Frank Mason, Aston Publications 1989
The Lancaster Story by Peter Jacobs, Arms & Armour Press 1996
Avro Lancaster by Ken Delve, Crowood Press 1999
Lancaster – Claims to Fame by Norman Franks, Arms & Armour 1994
Mynarski's Lanc – Canadian Warplane Heritage, Boston Mills Press Ontario 1989
G-for-George (Australian Lancaster) by Nelmes & Jenkins, Banner Books Queensland 2000

Associated books
Avro – The History of an Aircraft Company by Harry Holmes, Airlife 1994
Avro Manchester by Robert Kirby, Midland Publishing Limited 1995
Lincoln at War by Mike Garbett & Brian Goulding, Ian Allan 1979
Lancaster Target by Jack Currie, New English Library 1977
Lancaster to Berlin by Walter Thompson, Totem Books, Toronto 1985
The Salford Lancaster by Joe Bamford, Pen & Sword 1996
Luck and a Lancaster by Harry Yates, Airlife 1998
Tail Gunner by Chan Chandler, Airlife 1999
The Design & Development of the Avro Lancaster Royal Aeronautical Society, Manchester Branch 1991

Index

Page numbers in *italics* refer to illustrations.